AF687937

Thriving Within Your Means: A Guide to Affordable Living

Alex Thompson

Published by Side Hustle Success, 2023.

THRIVING WITHIN YOUR MEANS: A GUIDE TO AFFORDABLE LIVING

First edition. September 8, 2023.

ISBN: 979-8223056867

Written by Alex Thompson.

Table of Contents

This book is dedicated to all those who believe in the power of financial freedom and ethical living. To the dreamers, the savers, the doers, and the seekers of a better life—may you find inspiration, knowledge, and the path to affordable living within these pages.

Chapter 1: Introduction

Defining the Goal of Affordable Living: Achieving Financial Stability Legally and Ethically

In an era where housing costs often represent a significant portion of our monthly expenses, achieving affordable living is a goal that resonates with many. However, it's important to clarify the objective of affordable living from the outset: it's about achieving financial stability while staying well within the bounds of legality and ethics. In this introduction, we set the tone for our journey toward affordable living by defining this essential goal.

Financial Stability as the North Star

Financial stability is the ultimate aim of affordable living. But what exactly does it mean? At its core, financial stability entails having enough financial resources to meet your basic needs, secure your future, and comfortably navigate life's uncertainties. It means not constantly worrying about how to cover your housing costs, putting food on the table, or handling unexpected emergencies.

However, achieving financial stability doesn't imply extreme frugality, sacrificing your well-being, or resorting to dubious practices. It's about striking a balance between your income and expenses, making informed financial decisions, and ensuring that you're not burdened by excessive housing costs.

The Pitfalls of Unethical and Illegal Means

While the desire for affordable living is understandable, it's essential to stress that certain paths toward reducing housing costs, such as squatting, fraudulent activities, or exploiting legal loopholes unethically, are not only unsustainable but also illegal and harmful. Engaging in such practices can lead to severe legal consequences, tarnished reputations, and moral dilemmas.

In this book, we'll focus exclusively on strategies that are legal, ethical, and sustainable. We believe that true financial stability can only be achieved when your actions align with the principles of honesty, integrity, and legality. It's not just about saving money; it's about doing so while maintaining your moral compass and respecting the rights and well-being of others.

Why Pursue Affordable Living?

Before we embark on this journey, it's worth exploring why affordable living is a worthy pursuit. Affordable living offers a plethora of benefits:

1. **Financial Freedom**: Reducing housing costs liberates your income, allowing you to allocate it toward your financial goals, such as retirement savings, investments, or debt reduction.
2. **Reduced Stress**: Lower housing costs mean fewer financial worries, reducing stress and improving your overall well-being.
3. **Improved Financial Health**: It enables you to build a stronger financial foundation by saving and investing more of your income.
4. **Sustainability**: Sustainable living isn't just about protecting the environment; it's also about maintaining a lifestyle that you can sustain over the long term.
5. **Peace of Mind**: When your housing situation is financially stable and ethically sound, you can enjoy peace of mind knowing that you're on the right path to a secure future.

In this book, we will explore practical, legal, and ethical strategies for reducing housing costs, sharing insights, tips, and real-life examples to guide you on your journey to affordable living. Remember, it's not about cutting corners or taking shortcuts; it's about making informed choices that align with your financial goals and values. Let's embark on this journey together and work towards the financial stability you deserve.

Emphasizing Responsible Financial Management and Ethical Considerations

In our journey towards achieving affordable living, one crucial aspect that will be a constant thread throughout this book is the unwavering emphasis on responsible financial management and ethical considerations. These two pillars are the cornerstones of our approach to reducing housing costs while ensuring our actions are not only legal but also in line with the principles of integrity and ethical conduct.

The Power of Responsible Financial Management

Before we delve deeper into the strategies and tactics for making housing more affordable, let's examine why responsible financial management is fundamental:

1. **Financial Stability**: Responsible financial management ensures that you have a solid financial foundation. This means having an emergency fund, staying out of crippling debt, and saving for the future. These elements are crucial to achieving affordable living.
2. **Long-term Goals**: Effective financial management enables you to plan and work towards your long-term financial goals, whether it's buying a home, funding your children's education, or enjoying a comfortable retirement.
3. **Stress Reduction**: A well-managed financial life leads to reduced financial stress. This, in turn, improves your overall quality of life, health, and well-being.
4. **Smart Decision-Making**: Responsible financial management equips you with the tools and knowledge to make informed financial decisions. It empowers you to navigate complex financial landscapes confidently.

Throughout this book, we will provide practical guidance on budgeting, saving, investing, and managing debt. These skills are not only vital for achieving affordable living but also for building a secure financial future.

Ethical Considerations in Affordable Living

While the financial aspect is crucial, it's equally important to recognize the ethical dimensions of affordable living:

1. **Legal and Moral Obligations**: Ethical considerations remind us of our legal and moral obligations. This includes respecting property rights, adhering to contractual agreements, and treating others with

fairness and integrity.

2. **Community and Society**: Our actions in the pursuit of affordable living can impact the broader community and society. Engaging in unethical or illegal practices can harm others and erode the trust within our communities.
3. **Long-term Viability**: Unethical or illegal shortcuts may provide short-term gains, but they rarely lead to sustainable solutions. True affordable living is about creating a lifestyle that can be maintained over the long haul.
4. **Personal Integrity**: Lastly, ethical considerations tie directly to personal integrity. Making ethical choices in your financial life ensures that you remain true to your values and principles.

Throughout this book, we will explore strategies that are not only financially prudent but also ethically sound. This approach will not only help you reduce your housing costs but also maintain your personal integrity and respect for others.

As we proceed through the chapters, remember that the path to affordable living is not just about numbers and dollars; it's about aligning your financial choices with your values and ethics. We are here to guide you on this journey towards financial stability, responsible financial management, and ethical living. Together, we will explore practical, legal, and ethical strategies for achieving affordable living while maintaining your moral compass.

Highlighting the Benefits of Pursuing Affordable Living

As we embark on this journey towards affordable living with responsible financial management and ethical considerations at the forefront, it's essential to understand the numerous advantages that come with this pursuit. Affordable living isn't just about tightening your belt or cutting corners; it's about making informed choices that can significantly enhance your financial well-being and overall quality of life.

1. Increased Financial Security

Achieving affordable living directly translates to increased financial security. Here's how:

- **Emergency Fund**: By reducing housing costs and managing your finances wisely, you can build and maintain a robust emergency fund. This financial safety net provides peace of mind and protects you from unexpected expenses or emergencies without resorting to debt.
- **Debt Reduction**: Lower housing expenses free up money that can be used to pay down existing debts, ultimately reducing your financial liabilities. With less debt hanging over your head, your financial security improves.
- **Savings and Investments**: Affordability allows you to allocate more funds towards savings and investments, helping you build wealth over time. Investments provide opportunities for your money to grow, further enhancing your financial security.

2. Reduced Stress

Financial stress can be overwhelming and detrimental to both your mental and physical health. Pursuing affordable living can significantly reduce stress:

- **Peace of Mind**: Knowing that your housing situation is financially manageable alleviates a significant source of stress. You won't constantly worry about how to cover your rent or mortgage.
- **Improved Mental Health**: Reduced financial stress is associated with better mental health. You can focus on other aspects of your life without the constant burden of financial worries.
- **Enhanced Relationships**: Financial stress often spills over into personal relationships. By achieving affordability, you can strengthen your relationships and maintain a harmonious family life.

3. Improved Financial Health

Affordable living contributes to your overall financial health in several ways:

- **Savings Growth**: Lower housing expenses mean more money to save and invest, which is essential for long-term financial health. Your savings can be used for retirement, education, or other financial goals.
- **Debt Management**: With additional funds at your disposal, you can tackle high-interest debt more effectively, such as credit card debt. Reducing or eliminating debt is a crucial step toward financial health.
- **Asset Accumulation**: Over time, the ability to save and invest will lead to the accumulation of assets. This can include real estate investments, stocks, and other income-generating assets.

4. Sustainability

Affordable living promotes sustainability on multiple levels:

- **Financial Sustainability**: Living within your means and managing your finances responsibly ensures that your financial situation is sustainable over the long term.
- **Environmental Sustainability**: Some affordable living strategies, such as downsizing to a smaller home or adopting energy-efficient practices, can contribute to a more environmentally sustainable lifestyle.

5. Peace of Mind

Ultimately, the pursuit of affordable living offers peace of mind:

- **Reduced Financial Worries**: When your housing situation is secure and financially manageable, you can focus on your broader life goals and aspirations without the constant stress of financial concerns.
- **Confidence in the Future**: Achieving affordable living instills confidence in your financial future. You'll know that you're on the right path to a secure retirement, educational savings for your children, or any other financial goal you set.

In the chapters that follow, we will explore various strategies, techniques, and tips to help you achieve affordable living while reaping these benefits. Remember, it's not about making drastic sacrifices but rather about making informed choices that align with your financial goals and values. By pursuing affordable living with responsibility and ethics as your guiding principles, you can enjoy a more secure, less stressful, and financially fulfilling life.

Mentioning the Consequences of Illegal or Unethical Actions in Housing

While the pursuit of affordable living is undoubtedly a commendable goal, it's paramount to recognize the potential repercussions of engaging in illegal or unethical actions related to housing. These actions, although they may offer short-term gains, often lead to long-lasting, adverse consequences that can affect your legal standing and reputation. In this section, we'll shed light on these potential consequences, underscoring the importance of staying within legal and ethical boundaries.

Legal Penalties

Engaging in illegal housing practices can result in a range of legal consequences, including:

1. **Eviction**: If you occupy a property without the owner's consent or fail to pay rent, you could face eviction. This can lead to homelessness and damage to your rental history, making it challenging to secure future housing.
2. **Fines**: Many jurisdictions impose fines for illegal housing activities, such as squatting, fraudulent rental agreements, or occupancy violations.
3. **Criminal Charges**: Some actions related to housing can lead to criminal charges. For example, property fraud, identity theft, or housing scams can result in serious legal trouble.
4. **Civil Lawsuits**: Property owners may pursue civil lawsuits to recover unpaid rent or damages caused by illegal or unethical actions. These lawsuits can result in significant financial liabilities.
5. **Legal Records**: Criminal charges, eviction records, or court

judgments related to housing violations can become part of your legal record, affecting your future housing and employment prospects.

Reputation Damage

Beyond legal consequences, engaging in unethical or illegal housing practices can tarnish your reputation:

1. **Trustworthiness**: A history of unethical behavior in housing can damage your reputation as a trustworthy individual, making it challenging to establish trust in personal and professional relationships.
2. **Professional Consequences**: Reputation damage can spill over into your professional life. Employers may hesitate to hire or promote individuals with a history of unethical or criminal activities.
3. **Community Standing**: Your standing within your community can be negatively impacted. Word of your actions may spread, leading to social ostracization or strained relationships.
4. **Personal Stress**: The stress of engaging in unethical or illegal actions can take a toll on your mental and emotional well-being, affecting your overall quality of life.
5. **Legal Constraints**: Depending on the severity of your actions, legal restrictions such as probation or parole may limit your personal and professional freedoms.

In this book, we are committed to guiding you towards affordable living through legal, ethical, and sustainable means. We firmly believe that the pursuit of financial stability should never come at the expense of integrity, legality, or the well-being of others. Our focus is on strategies and practices that not only reduce your housing costs but also uphold your reputation and legal standing. By choosing the path of ethical and legal actions, you can achieve affordable living while safeguarding your future and your personal integrity.

Setting the Tone: A Guide to Practical, Legal, and Ethical Strategies for Reducing Housing Expenses

As we embark on this journey towards affordable living, it is crucial to establish the tone and framework that will guide us throughout this book. Our mission is clear: to equip you with the knowledge, tools, and strategies necessary to reduce your housing expenses while adhering unwaveringly to principles of practicality, legality, and ethics.

Practicality as the Foundation

At the heart of this book lies practicality—a commitment to providing you with real-world solutions that are actionable and effective. Our aim is to offer strategies that fit seamlessly into your life, regardless of your income level or living situation. We understand that the pursuit of affordable living should not entail extraordinary sacrifices or discomfort. Instead, it's about making informed, practical choices that align with your financial goals and values.

Legality as the Cornerstone

Legality is non-negotiable in our approach. Affordable living should never come at the expense of breaking the law or violating legal agreements. We will explore strategies that are not only effective but also fully compliant with local, state, and national laws. Our commitment to legality ensures that your pursuit of affordable living remains free from the risk of legal consequences and safeguards your long-term financial well-being.

Ethics as the Guiding Light

Ethical considerations are embedded in every facet of this book. We firmly believe that the pursuit of financial stability should always be conducted with the utmost integrity and respect for others. Our strategies prioritize ethical conduct, ensuring that your actions align with the principles of fairness, honesty, and responsibility. By choosing ethical paths to affordable living, you can achieve your financial goals without compromising your personal integrity.

What to Expect in This Book

Throughout the chapters that follow, we will provide you with a comprehensive toolkit for reducing housing expenses while upholding the principles of practicality, legality, and ethics. You will discover:

- **Budgeting Techniques**: Practical methods for creating and sticking to a budget that works for you, helping you regain control of your finances.
- **Negotiation Strategies**: Legal and ethical ways to negotiate rent, mortgage rates, or other housing-related costs, enabling you to secure better deals.
- **Alternative Housing Options**: A diverse range of housing alternatives that can significantly reduce your living expenses without resorting to illegal or unethical practices.
- **Income-Generating Ideas**: Passive income streams and investment strategies to complement your financial stability while maintaining ethical standards.
- **Community Resources and Support**: A wealth of community resources that can provide you with valuable assistance on your journey towards affordable living.

In each chapter, we will delve into these topics, providing you with practical advice, actionable steps, and real-life examples that illustrate the power of practical, legal, and ethical approaches to affordable living.

Our commitment to your financial well-being and ethical conduct remains unwavering. By the end of this book, you will be equipped not only with the knowledge to reduce your housing expenses but also with the wisdom to make financial decisions that reflect your values and respect for others. Together, let's embark on this journey towards affordable living, where practicality, legality, and ethics pave the path to financial freedom and peace of mind.

Chapter 2: Budgeting and Financial Management

Explaining the Process of Creating a Detailed Budget, Including Tracking Income and Expenses

Budgeting is the cornerstone of responsible financial management and a crucial tool in our journey toward affordable living. A well-structured budget empowers you to take control of your finances, allocate resources wisely, and work towards your financial goals. In this chapter, we will break down the process of creating a detailed budget, which includes tracking both income and expenses.

1. Assess Your Financial Situation

Before you dive into budgeting, it's essential to understand your current financial situation. This involves:

- **Income Evaluation**: Calculate your total monthly income from all sources, including your salary, side gigs, rental income, and any other inflows of money.
- **Expense Review**: Examine your recent expenses, ideally over the last few months. Categorize them into fixed expenses (e.g., rent or mortgage, utilities) and variable expenses (e.g., groceries, entertainment). This step provides a clear picture of your spending habits.

2. Set Clear Financial Goals

What are you trying to achieve with your budget? Are you saving for a down payment on a home, paying off debt, or building an emergency fund? Setting specific, measurable, achievable, relevant, and time-bound (SMART) financial goals helps you stay motivated and focused.

3. Create Categories and Allocate Funds

Divide your expenses into categories such as housing, transportation, food, entertainment, and savings. Allocate a specific amount of money to each category based on your financial goals and priorities. This step ensures that you're controlling your spending in each area.

4. Track Your Spending

Once your budget is set, diligently track your spending against the allocated amounts. You can use various tools for this, including budgeting apps, spreadsheets, or even pen and paper. Recording every expense, no matter how small, is critical for gaining insights into your financial behavior.

5. Review and Adjust Regularly

Budgeting isn't a one-time task; it's an ongoing process. Regularly review your budget to assess your progress and make necessary adjustments. Life is dynamic, and unexpected expenses may arise. By routinely evaluating and adapting your budget, you can stay on course.

6. Build an Emergency Fund

An essential part of your budget is setting aside funds for emergencies. Financial experts recommend having at least three to six months' worth of living expenses saved in case of unexpected events like medical bills, car repairs, or job loss.

7. Prioritize Debt Management

If you have outstanding debts, allocate a portion of your budget to paying them down. Focus on high-interest debts first while making minimum payments on others. Reducing debt is a significant step toward financial stability.

8. Automate Savings and Bill Payments

Make the budgeting process easier by automating savings and bill payments. Set up automatic transfers to your savings account and automate your regular bills. This ensures that you're consistently saving and paying your obligations on time.

9. Stay Disciplined and Adjust as Needed

Budgeting requires discipline, but it shouldn't be overly restrictive. It's essential to maintain a balance between responsible financial management and enjoying your life. If you find yourself consistently overspending in a category, consider adjusting your budget to reflect your actual habits while keeping your financial goals in mind.

Creating a detailed budget and tracking income and expenses isn't just about numbers; it's about gaining control over your finances and making informed decisions. As you progress through this book, you'll find additional strategies and tips that will complement your budgeting efforts, helping you achieve your financial goals and ultimately attain affordable living while staying within legal and ethical boundaries.

Tips for Setting Financial Goals and Creating a Savings Plan

Setting clear financial goals and establishing a savings plan are pivotal steps in the journey toward affordable living. Without a roadmap for your finances, it's easy to lose track and become overwhelmed by day-to-day expenses. In this section, we will offer valuable tips to help you set meaningful financial goals and create a savings plan that aligns with your objectives.

Setting Financial Goals:

1. **Be Specific**: Define your financial goals with precision. Vague goals like "save more money" are less effective than specific goals like "save $10,000 for a down payment on a home by December 31, 20XX."
2. **Make Them Measurable**: Ensure that your goals are quantifiable. This enables you to track your progress and know when you've achieved them. For example, "pay off $5,000 in credit card debt within one year."
3. **Consider Short-Term and Long-Term Goals**: Balance your financial goals between short-term objectives (e.g., building an emergency fund) and long-term aspirations (e.g., retirement savings). This diversification keeps your financial journey dynamic and motivating.
4. **Prioritize**: Identify which goals are most urgent and important to

you. This will help you allocate your resources and time effectively. Some goals, such as paying off high-interest debt, may take precedence over others.

5. **Make Them Achievable**: Ensure that your goals are realistic given your current financial situation. While ambitious goals are admirable, setting unattainable ones can lead to discouragement.
6. **Time-Bound**: Assign a timeframe to each goal. This creates a sense of urgency and helps you stay accountable. For example, "save $500 for a weekend getaway in six months."

Creating a Savings Plan:

1. **Establish an Emergency Fund**: Your first savings priority should be an emergency fund. Aim to save at least three to six months' worth of living expenses. This fund provides a financial safety net for unexpected events.
2. **Automate Savings**: Set up automatic transfers from your checking account to your savings account. This "pay yourself first" approach ensures that saving becomes a consistent habit.
3. **Use Separate Savings Accounts**: Consider having multiple savings accounts for different goals. For example, you might have one for emergencies, one for a vacation fund, and another for a down payment on a home.
4. **Track and Review Progress**: Regularly monitor your savings goals. Use budgeting tools or apps to keep tabs on your progress. Review your goals periodically and adjust them as needed.
5. **Cut Unnecessary Expenses**: Identify areas in your budget where you can cut back on expenses. Redirect the money you save into your savings goals. Small sacrifices in discretionary spending can add up over time.
6. **Increase Your Income**: Look for opportunities to boost your income, such as part-time work, freelance gigs, or selling unused items. The additional income can accelerate your savings plan.
7. **Take Advantage of Employer Benefits**: If your employer offers retirement accounts with matching contributions, take full advantage

of this benefit. It's essentially free money that can help you achieve long-term savings goals.

8. **Consider Tax-Advantaged Accounts**: Explore tax-advantaged accounts like 401(k)s, IRAs, or Health Savings Accounts (HSAs) to maximize your savings and minimize tax liabilities.
9. **Be Patient and Stay Disciplined**: Building savings takes time and discipline. There will be periods of slow progress, but consistency is key. Stay focused on your goals and avoid dipping into your savings for non-essential expenses.

Remember, your savings plan is a dynamic tool that can adapt to your changing financial circumstances. By setting clear, achievable goals and consistently saving toward them, you'll not only make affordable living a reality but also build a strong financial foundation for the future.

Discussing the Importance of Emergency Funds and How They Prevent Financial Crises

One of the foundational elements of responsible financial management and achieving affordable living is the establishment of an emergency fund. Emergency funds serve as a financial safety net, providing protection against unexpected expenses and preventing financial crises. In this section, we will delve into the significance of emergency funds and how they can safeguard your financial stability.

The Significance of Emergency Funds:

1. **Financial Security**: An emergency fund provides a sense of financial security. Knowing that you have readily accessible funds in case of unexpected expenses reduces anxiety and stress associated with financial uncertainty.
2. **Protection Against the Unexpected**: Life is filled with unforeseen events, such as medical emergencies, car repairs, or unexpected job loss. An emergency fund ensures that you're prepared to handle these unexpected situations without resorting to high-interest loans or credit cards.

3. **Avoiding Debt**: Without an emergency fund, many people turn to credit cards or loans to cover unforeseen expenses. This can lead to a cycle of debt that's challenging to break. An emergency fund helps you avoid accumulating high-interest debt.
4. **Maintaining Financial Goals**: Unexpected expenses can derail your progress toward other financial goals, such as saving for a home, retirement, or education. An emergency fund ensures that these goals remain intact, even in the face of adversity.
5. **Opportunity to Invest**: When you have an emergency fund, you can confidently invest in opportunities that may arise, such as a good investment deal or a career advancement that requires some initial expenses.

How Emergency Funds Prevent Financial Crises:

1. **Immediate Access to Funds**: With an emergency fund in place, you have immediate access to cash when you need it most. You can cover essential expenses without delay.
2. **No Need for High-Interest Borrowing**: Instead of relying on high-interest loans or credit cards, you can use your emergency fund to handle unexpected expenses. This prevents the accumulation of costly debt.
3. **Peace of Mind**: The mere presence of an emergency fund offers peace of mind. Financial crises are less daunting when you know you have the resources to handle them.
4. **Preservation of Financial Health**: Emergency funds act as a buffer that preserves your overall financial health. You can weather financial storms without significantly impacting your long-term financial well-being.

Building and Maintaining an Emergency Fund:

1. **Set a Goal**: Determine how much you want to save in your emergency fund. A common guideline is three to six months' worth of living expenses, but your situation may require more or less.

2. **Consistent Contributions**: Regularly contribute to your emergency fund, even if it's a small amount at first. Consistency is more important than the initial sum.
3. **Automate Savings**: Automate transfers from your checking account to your emergency fund to ensure that saving becomes a habit.
4. **Use Windfalls Wisely**: Allocate unexpected windfalls, such as tax refunds or work bonuses, to your emergency fund to accelerate its growth.
5. **Avoid Temptation**: Commit to using your emergency fund only for genuine emergencies. Avoid tapping into it for non-essential expenses.
6. **Regularly Review and Adjust**: Periodically assess your emergency fund's balance and make adjustments based on changes in your financial situation and goals.

In summary, an emergency fund serves as a crucial financial cushion, shielding you from unexpected expenses and preventing financial crises. By consistently contributing to and maintaining your emergency fund, you can enjoy peace of mind, protect your financial health, and stay on track towards affordable living while adhering to practical, legal, and ethical principles.

Strategies for Managing Debt and Improving Credit Scores

Debt management and credit score improvement are integral components of responsible financial management, and they play a significant role in achieving affordable living. In this section, we'll explore effective strategies to help you manage your debt effectively and work towards improving your credit scores.

Debt Management Strategies:

1. **Create a Debt Repayment Plan**: Start by listing all your debts, including outstanding balances, interest rates, and minimum monthly payments. Create a debt repayment plan that outlines how you'll tackle your debts systematically.
2. **Prioritize High-Interest Debt**: Focus on paying off high-interest debts first, such as credit card balances. These debts accumulate

interest rapidly and can be a significant drain on your finances.

3. **Consider Debt Consolidation**: Explore debt consolidation options, such as transferring high-interest credit card debt to a lower-interest card or consolidating multiple debts into a single loan. This can simplify your payments and reduce overall interest costs.
4. **Negotiate with Creditors**: If you're struggling to make payments, don't hesitate to negotiate with your creditors. They may be willing to work out a more manageable repayment plan or offer temporary relief.
5. **Live Within Your Means**: Adjust your spending habits to ensure that you can cover your basic living expenses and make debt payments. Avoid accruing more debt while you work on paying down existing balances.

Credit Score Improvement Strategies:

1. **Check Your Credit Report**: Obtain a free copy of your credit report from each of the major credit bureaus (Equifax, Experian, and TransUnion) annually. Review your reports for errors or discrepancies and dispute any inaccuracies.
2. **Pay Bills On Time**: Consistently paying bills, loans, and credit card payments on time is one of the most significant factors in determining your credit score. Set up reminders or automatic payments to avoid late payments.
3. **Reduce Credit Card Balances**: Aim to keep your credit card balances well below your credit limits. High credit card utilization can negatively impact your credit score.
4. **Diversify Your Credit Mix**: Having a mix of different types of credit accounts, such as credit cards, installment loans, and a mortgage, can positively affect your credit score. However, only open new credit accounts when necessary.
5. **Avoid Closing Old Accounts**: Closing old credit card accounts can shorten your credit history, potentially lowering your credit score. Keep older accounts open, even if you don't use them frequently.
6. **Limit New Credit Applications**: Each time you apply for credit, it

can result in a hard inquiry on your credit report, which can temporarily lower your score. Be selective about new credit applications.

7. **Use Credit Responsibly**: Demonstrating responsible credit use over time can improve your credit score. This includes paying off balances, managing credit limits, and avoiding excessive debt.
8. **Seek Professional Help if Needed**: If you're struggling with severe credit issues, consider seeking assistance from a reputable credit counseling agency or a financial advisor who specializes in credit repair.

Managing debt and improving your credit score require patience and discipline. By implementing these strategies, you can work toward reducing financial burdens, securing better lending terms, and ultimately enhancing your financial well-being. As you progress through this book, you'll discover more insights and techniques that complement your journey towards affordable living while upholding ethical and legal standards.

Recommendations for Maintaining a Healthy Financial Lifestyle

Maintaining a healthy financial lifestyle is essential for long-term financial stability and achieving affordable living. Beyond budgeting, debt management, and credit score improvement, there are broader recommendations that can guide your overall financial approach. These recommendations encompass responsible financial habits and ethical considerations:

1. Regularly Review and Update Your Financial Goals:

- Periodically assess your financial objectives and adjust them as your life circumstances change. This ensures that your goals remain relevant and motivating.

2. Build and Maintain an Emergency Fund:

- Continue to contribute to your emergency fund, even after reaching your initial savings goal. As your expenses or income change, adjust the fund's size accordingly.

3. Prioritize Retirement Savings:

- Contribute consistently to retirement accounts, taking full advantage of employer matches and exploring tax-advantaged options like IRAs and 401(k)s.

4. Diversify Your Investments:

- Diversification can help reduce risk in your investment portfolio. Consult with a financial advisor to create a well-balanced investment strategy.

5. Educate Yourself Continuously:

- Stay informed about personal finance trends, investment opportunities, and financial literacy. Read books, follow reputable financial news sources, and consider financial education courses.

6. Avoid Lifestyle Inflation:

- As your income increases, resist the temptation to inflate your lifestyle proportionally. Instead, allocate the extra income towards savings, investments, or debt reduction.

7. Be Cautious with Large Purchases:

- Before making significant purchases, like a car or home, thoroughly research your options, negotiate prices, and assess the long-term financial impact.

8. Maintain Ethical Conduct:

- Uphold ethical principles in all your financial dealings. Honesty, integrity, and responsibility should guide your actions, whether in business, investments, or personal finance.

9. Give Back to the Community:

- Consider allocating a portion of your income or time to charitable endeavors or community service. Giving back can enrich your life while supporting causes you believe in.

10. Avoid Comparisons:

- Avoid comparing your financial situation to others'. Everyone's financial journey is unique, and external comparisons can lead to unnecessary stress or poor financial decisions.

11. Review Insurance Coverage:

- Regularly review your insurance policies to ensure they align with your current needs and circumstances. This includes health, auto, home, and life insurance.

12. Seek Professional Advice When Necessary:

- Don't hesitate to consult with financial professionals, such as financial advisors, accountants, or estate planners, for expert guidance on complex financial matters.

13. Stay Mindful of Taxes:

- Explore tax-efficient strategies to minimize your tax liability legally. This includes taking advantage of tax deductions, credits, and tax-advantaged accounts.

14. Promote Financial Literacy:

- Share your financial knowledge and experiences with friends and family to promote financial literacy within your community.

15. Celebrate Milestones:

- Acknowledge and celebrate your financial achievements, both big and small. Positive reinforcement can help maintain motivation on your financial journey.

Maintaining a healthy financial lifestyle requires continuous effort, adaptability, and a commitment to ethical conduct. By incorporating these recommendations into your financial approach, you can build a strong foundation for affordable living while enhancing your overall financial well-being. As you progress through this book, you'll gain additional insights and strategies to support your journey toward financial stability and ethical living.

Chapter 3: Reducing Housing Costs

Describing Effective Negotiation Techniques for Lowering Rent with Your Landlord

Negotiating a lower rent with your landlord is a valuable skill that can significantly contribute to achieving affordable living. Whether you're signing a new lease or renewing an existing one, employing effective negotiation techniques can help you secure a more favorable rental rate. Here's a step-by-step guide on how to negotiate your rent:

1. Do Your Homework:

- Research the local rental market to understand current trends and average rental prices for similar properties in your area. Having this information will provide you with a solid foundation for negotiations.

2. Time Your Negotiation:

- Choose the right time to negotiate. Ideally, start the conversation a few months before your lease is up for renewal or during a period of low demand in the rental market. Landlords may be more open to negotiations when they have vacant units.

3. Be a Good Tenant:

- Prior to negotiating, ensure that you have been a responsible tenant. Pay your rent on time, maintain the property, and adhere to the terms of your lease. A good track record can strengthen your bargaining position.

4. Develop a Strong Argument:

- Identify valid reasons for requesting a rent reduction. For instance, you can mention any maintenance issues that need attention, improvements you've made to the property, or the fact that you've been a long-term tenant who pays rent reliably.

5. Practice Effective Communication:

- Approach your landlord with respect and professionalism. Clearly articulate your request and explain the reasons behind it. Be prepared to negotiate politely and patiently.

6. Offer a Win-Win Proposal:

- Propose a reasonable reduction in rent that aligns with current market rates but also considers your landlord's financial interests. Highlight how this reduction can benefit both parties. For instance, you could mention that a lower rent would encourage you to stay longer, reducing tenant turnover costs for the landlord.

7. Be Willing to Compromise:

- Be prepared for some back-and-forth with your landlord. They may counteroffer with a smaller reduction or other concessions. Be open to compromise to reach a mutually beneficial agreement.

8. Get It in Writing:

- Once you and your landlord agree on a new rent amount, ensure that the terms are documented in writing. This should include the new rental rate, the duration of the agreement, and any other agreed-upon terms.

9. Be Prepared to Walk Away:

- If negotiations do not yield a satisfactory outcome, be ready to explore other housing options. Sometimes, landlords may not be willing to reduce rent, and it's essential to consider alternatives.

10. Know Your Rights:

- Familiarize yourself with tenant rights and local rental laws to ensure that your request for a rent reduction is within legal boundaries. This knowledge can also be a valuable resource during negotiations.

11. Consider Long-Term Solutions:

- In addition to negotiating rent, explore the possibility of a longer-term lease, which can provide stability and potentially lock in a lower rate for an extended period.

12. Keep the Lines of Communication Open:

- Maintain a positive relationship with your landlord throughout the negotiation process. Clear and open communication can lead to better outcomes.

Negotiating rent is a skill that can yield substantial savings over time. By approaching the negotiation process with research, professionalism, and a willingness to compromise, you can increase your chances of achieving a more affordable living situation while maintaining a respectful and ethical relationship with your landlord.

Explaining the Process of Refinancing a Mortgage to Secure a Lower Interest Rate or Monthly Payment

Refinancing a mortgage is a strategic move that can lead to substantial savings by securing a lower interest rate or reducing your monthly mortgage payment. This process involves replacing your current mortgage with a new one under improved terms. Here's a step-by-step guide on how to refinance your mortgage effectively:

1. Evaluate Your Financial Situation:

- Before considering refinancing, assess your current financial situation, credit score, and goals. Determine why you want to refinance—whether it's to reduce monthly payments, shorten the loan term, or tap into home equity.

2. Check Your Credit Score:

- A good credit score is crucial for securing a lower interest rate during the refinancing process. Review your credit report and address any errors or issues that could negatively impact your score.

3. Research Mortgage Rates:

- Monitor current mortgage rates and market conditions. Timing is essential; you'll want to refinance when rates are favorable to maximize your savings.

4. Gather Financial Documents:

- Prepare necessary financial documents, including pay stubs, tax returns, bank statements, and proof of assets. These will be required during the application process.

5. Estimate Refinancing Costs:

- Understand the costs associated with refinancing, which may include application fees, appraisal fees, closing costs, and points. Calculate how long it will take to recoup these costs through reduced monthly payments.

6. Compare Lenders:

- Shop around and compare offers from various lenders, including banks, credit unions, and online mortgage lenders. Each may have different rates, terms, and fees.

7. Get Preapproved:

- Once you identify a lender, start the preapproval process. This involves submitting your financial documents and having the lender review your creditworthiness.

8. Select a Mortgage Product:

- Choose the type of mortgage that best suits your needs. Common options include fixed-rate mortgages (which offer a stable interest rate) and adjustable-rate mortgages (which have variable interest rates).

9. Lock in the Rate:

- Once you're satisfied with the lender's terms and rates, request a rate lock. This ensures that the interest rate remains the same during the loan approval process.

10. Complete the Application:

- Submit a formal loan application to the chosen lender. Be prepared to provide detailed financial information, including income, expenses, and employment history.

11. Appraisal and Inspection:

- The lender may require a home appraisal and inspection to assess the property's value and condition. These steps are essential in determining the new loan amount.

12. Underwriting and Approval:

- The lender's underwriting team will review your application, financial documents, and property appraisal. If everything aligns with their criteria, they will approve the loan.

13. Closing the Loan:

- Schedule a closing date to sign the final loan documents. Be prepared to pay closing costs and any upfront fees.

14. Review the New Loan Terms:

- Carefully examine the terms of the new mortgage, including the interest rate, monthly payment, and loan duration. Ensure that they align with your refinancing goals.

15. Close on the New Mortgage:

- Sign the closing documents in the presence of a notary public or closing agent. Afterward, the new mortgage will replace your old one, and you'll begin making payments according to the new terms.

16. Continue Monitoring Rates:

- Even after refinancing, stay vigilant about mortgage rates. If rates drop significantly in the future, you might consider refinancing again to secure even better terms.

17. Use Savings Wisely:

- Consider your financial goals for the extra funds saved through refinancing. You might use the savings to pay down debt, invest, or build an emergency fund.

Refinancing a mortgage can be a strategic move to reduce housing costs and improve your financial stability. By carefully following these steps and seeking the guidance of a trusted mortgage professional, you can navigate the refinancing process effectively and secure a mortgage that better aligns with your financial goals.

Highlighting Government Assistance Programs and How to Apply for Section 8 Housing Vouchers

Government assistance programs, such as Section 8 Housing Choice Vouchers, can provide valuable support to individuals and families struggling with housing costs. These programs aim to make housing more affordable by subsidizing rental payments. Here's an overview of Section 8 and how to apply for these vouchers:

Section 8 Housing Choice Vouchers:

What Is Section 8?

- Section 8 is a federal housing program administered by the U.S. Department of Housing and Urban Development (HUD). It assists low-income individuals and families in securing safe and affordable housing in the private rental market.

How Do Section 8 Vouchers Work?

- Recipients of Section 8 vouchers are responsible for finding suitable, privately-owned rental housing. The program subsidizes a portion of the rent, making it more affordable for tenants. Recipients typically pay around 30% of their income toward rent, with the voucher covering the rest.

Eligibility for Section 8:

- Eligibility for Section 8 is primarily based on income, family size, and U.S. citizenship or eligible immigration status. To qualify, your income must fall below a certain threshold, which varies by location. Generally, applicants with lower incomes receive higher priority.

How to Apply for Section 8 Housing Choice Vouchers:

1. Locate Your Local Public Housing Agency (PHA):

- PHAs are responsible for administering Section 8 vouchers at the local level. Use the HUD website or contact HUD's Public Housing Customer Service to find the PHA serving your area.

2. Determine Eligibility:

- Review the PHA's specific eligibility criteria and income limits. Ensure that you meet these requirements before applying.

3. Complete the Application:

- Obtain a Section 8 Housing Choice Voucher application from your local PHA. Some PHAs offer online applications, while others require you to pick up a physical form.

4. Gather Required Documentation:

- Prepare the necessary documentation, which typically includes proof of income, identification, and other supporting documents specified by the PHA.

5. Submit the Application:

- Submit your completed application and all required documents to your local PHA within the designated timeframe. Be sure to keep copies of your application and documents for your records.

6. Attend an Interview (If Required):

- Some PHAs may require applicants to attend an interview as part of the application process. Be prepared to discuss your housing needs and provide additional information.

7. Wait for Notification:

- After submitting your application, you'll need to wait for the PHA to review and process it. If you meet the eligibility criteria and there are available vouchers, you will receive notification about your Section 8 voucher status.

8. Search for Housing:

- Once you receive a Section 8 voucher, you can start searching for eligible rental housing in the private market. Your PHA may provide resources or listings to assist in your search.

9. Inspect and Approve the Property:

- Before moving in, the PHA will inspect the rental property to ensure it meets housing quality standards. Once approved, you can sign the lease and begin using your voucher.

10. Pay Your Portion of Rent:

- As a Section 8 voucher holder, you'll pay your portion of the rent directly to the landlord, while the PHA will send the rental assistance payment to the landlord on your behalf.

Remember that Section 8 vouchers are in high demand, and waiting lists may be long. It's essential to apply as soon as possible and follow up with the PHA regularly to check the status of your application. Additionally, be prepared for potential income verifications and eligibility updates throughout your participation in the program. Section 8 Housing Choice Vouchers can be a valuable resource for reducing housing costs and achieving affordable living for eligible individuals and families.

Discussing Downsizing Options and the Benefits of Living in a Smaller Space

Downsizing, or moving to a smaller living space, can be a strategic choice to reduce housing costs and achieve more affordable living. This chapter explores downsizing options and the numerous benefits of living in a smaller space:

1. Apartment Living:

- Apartments are a popular downsizing choice, offering various sizes and styles to suit different needs and budgets. They often come with amenities like fitness centers, laundry facilities, and maintenance services, reducing the need for personal upkeep.

2. Condominiums (Condos):

- Condos combine homeownership with shared amenities and maintenance responsibilities. They can be more affordable than single-family homes and often provide a sense of community.

3. Tiny Homes:

- Tiny homes are compact dwellings typically under 500 square feet. They offer an environmentally friendly and minimalist lifestyle, with lower utility and maintenance costs.

4. Downsizing Within a Home:

- If you're not ready to move, consider downsizing within your current home. Unused rooms can be repurposed or rented out to generate additional income.

Benefits of Living in a Smaller Space:

1. Reduced Housing Costs:

- Smaller spaces generally come with lower mortgage or rent payments, property taxes, and utility bills, allowing you to allocate more funds toward other financial goals.

2. Lower Maintenance and Upkeep:

- Smaller spaces require less maintenance and cleaning, saving you time and money. There's less space to repair or renovate, reducing the need for costly home improvements.

3. Simplified Lifestyle:

- Downsizing often encourages a simpler, more minimalistic lifestyle. You'll likely need to declutter and prioritize essentials, which can lead to reduced spending and less stress.

4. Environmental Impact:

- Smaller living spaces typically have a smaller carbon footprint. They require less energy for heating, cooling, and lighting, contributing to environmental sustainability.

5. Financial Freedom:

- Living in a smaller space can free up funds for other financial goals, such as saving for retirement, paying off debt, or investing. It provides more financial flexibility.

6. Less Clutter:

- Downsizing forces you to declutter and make conscious choices about your belongings. This can lead to a more organized and clutter-free living environment.

7. Closer Community:

- Smaller living spaces, such as apartments or condos, often promote a sense of community. You may have more opportunities to socialize with neighbors and build meaningful connections.

8. Mobility and Flexibility:

- Downsizing can make it easier to relocate if necessary, whether for job opportunities or personal reasons. Smaller spaces are typically more manageable to move out of.

9. Reduced Stress:

- With fewer possessions and less space to manage, you may experience reduced stress and an improved overall sense of well-being.

10. Focus on Experiences: - Living in a smaller space can shift your focus away from material possessions and towards experiences and relationships, leading to a more fulfilling life.

11. Environmental Consciousness: - Smaller living spaces often encourage environmentally responsible choices, such as energy-efficient appliances and sustainable living practices.

Ultimately, downsizing is a personal decision that should align with your lifestyle, goals, and preferences. It offers numerous financial and lifestyle benefits, making it a viable option for those seeking to reduce housing costs and pursue a more affordable and sustainable way of living.

Offering Guidance on Finding and Selecting Reliable Roommates to Share Housing Costs

Sharing housing costs with roommates is a practical way to reduce expenses and achieve affordable living. However, finding and selecting reliable roommates requires careful consideration to ensure a harmonious living arrangement. Here's a detailed guide to help you navigate this process effectively:

1. Determine Your Needs and Preferences:

Before you begin the process of finding and selecting roommates, it's essential to have a clear understanding of your own needs and preferences. Start by asking yourself some fundamental questions:

- What type of housing are you looking for (apartment, house, condominium, etc.)?
- What is your budget for rent and utilities?
- Are you open to living with individuals of any gender or specific preferences?
- Do you have any specific requirements regarding lifestyle, cleanliness, or habits?

- Are there any deal-breakers or absolute must-haves for your living situation?

By establishing a clear picture of your needs and preferences, you'll be better equipped to find roommates who align with your goals and living style.

2. Create a Clear Budget:

Financial considerations play a significant role in shared housing. It's crucial to establish a clear budget that outlines all of your monthly housing costs, including:

- Rent or mortgage payment
- Utilities (electricity, water, gas, internet, etc.)
- Groceries and household supplies
- Miscellaneous shared expenses (cleaning supplies, common area furnishings, etc.)

By calculating your total housing budget, you'll have a better understanding of how much each roommate should contribute. This information will be valuable when discussing finances with potential roommates.

3. Advertise for Roommates:

Once you've defined your needs and budget, it's time to start the search for potential roommates. There are various platforms and methods you can use to find roommates:

- **Online Listings**: Websites like Craigslist, Roommates.com, and Facebook Groups dedicated to housing can be excellent resources for finding roommates.
- **Social Media**: You can use your social media networks to spread the word that you're looking for roommates. This can be an effective way to find people within your circle of friends or acquaintances.
- **Local Classified Ads**: Many newspapers and community bulletin boards still host classified ads for housing. Check local publications

or community centers for these listings.

- **University or Workplace Bulletins**: If you're a student or working in a specific organization, check bulletin boards or online platforms dedicated to students or employees. These are often reliable sources for finding roommates who share similar schedules or interests.

When creating your roommate search listing, be sure to include all essential details about the property, including the location, size of the space, and any rules or expectations you have. Be honest and transparent to attract potential roommates who are genuinely interested and compatible.

4. Screen Potential Roommates:

As potential roommates express interest in your listing, it's time to start the screening process. Here's a comprehensive approach to screening potential roommates:

a. Conduct Interviews: Schedule interviews with potential roommates, either in person or via video chat. This initial conversation allows you to get to know each other and discuss essential details.

b. Income and Employment: One of the most critical factors to consider is the financial stability of potential roommates. Ask about their employment status, monthly income, and job stability. Ideally, roommates should have a stable source of income that can cover their share of the rent and expenses.

c. Rental History: Inquire about their rental history, including previous addresses and any issues they may have had with landlords or roommates. Request references from previous landlords if possible.

d. Lifestyle and Habits: Discuss lifestyle preferences and habits, such as cleanliness, smoking, pets, and daily routines. Make sure your potential roommates' lifestyles align with your own to minimize potential conflicts.

e. Compatibility: Ask about their expectations for shared living arrangements. Are they comfortable with the house rules and responsibilities you've outlined? Ensure that you share common values and expectations for the living situation.

f. Communication Skills: Assess their communication skills and willingness to resolve conflicts through open and respectful communication. Effective communication is key to maintaining a harmonious living environment.

g. Trust Your Instincts: Trust your intuition during the interview process. If something doesn't feel right or if you have any doubts about a potential roommate, it's essential to address these concerns.

5. Check References:

Request references from potential roommates to gain insights into their rental history and living habits. Contact previous landlords or roommates to inquire about their experiences with the applicant. Ask specific questions about rent payment consistency, cleanliness, and any conflicts that may have arisen.

References can provide valuable information and help you make an informed decision. Be sure to follow up on references promptly to keep the screening process moving smoothly.

6. Set Clear Expectations:

Clear and open communication is vital when living with roommates. Before finalizing your decision, engage in candid discussions about shared expectations. Topics to cover include:

- **Rent and Bill Payment**: Agree on how rent and bills will be divided and paid. Determine the due dates and preferred payment methods.
- **House Rules**: Establish clear house rules regarding cleanliness, quiet hours, guests, and any specific preferences or restrictions you may have.
- **Chores and Responsibilities**: Discuss how household chores and responsibilities will be divided. This includes tasks like cleaning, grocery shopping, and maintenance.
- **Privacy**: Respect each other's need for privacy and personal space. Define boundaries and discuss how to handle shared spaces.

7. Draft a Roommate Agreement:

A roommate agreement is a legally non-binding document that outlines the terms and expectations of shared living. While not legally enforceable, it can serve as a reference point and help prevent conflicts. Include the following elements in your roommate agreement:

- Full names and contact information of all roommates
- Address and description of the rental property
- Rent payment details, including the total rent, each roommate's share, and due dates
- Utility bill payment details
- House rules and expectations for shared living
- Chores and responsibilities
- Guidelines for handling disputes or conflicts
- Termination and move-out procedures

Have all roommates review and sign the roommate agreement, and provide each roommate with a copy for reference.

8. Verify Financial Responsibility:

Before finalizing your decision, it's crucial to verify the financial responsibility of potential roommates. Ensure that they have a stable source of income and can comfortably afford their share of the rent and utilities. Request proof of income or employment, such as recent pay stubs or a letter from their employer.

Financial stability is a crucial factor in preventing financial disputes or missed rent payments in the future.

9. Conduct an In-Person Meeting:

Whenever possible, arrange an in-person meeting with potential roommates before making a final decision. Meeting face-to-face allows you to gauge their personality, communication style, and overall compatibility. It also provides an opportunity to tour the living space together and discuss any questions or concerns.

10. Consider Compatibility:

Compatibility is a key factor in ensuring a harmonious living situation. While it's not necessary to have identical lifestyles or interests, there should be a degree of compatibility to promote a positive living environment. Consider the following factors:

- Daily routines and schedules
- Social preferences (introverted vs. extroverted)
- Dietary preferences and habits
- Attitudes toward cleanliness and organization
- Noise tolerance and preferences for quiet hours

While differences can add diversity to your living situation, it's essential to have a shared understanding and respect for each other's preferences and habits.

11. Discuss Emergency Plans:

Before finalizing your decision to live with roommates, it's wise to discuss emergency plans and procedures. These include how to handle unexpected situations such as:

- Repairs and maintenance issues
- Unexpected expenses (e.g., major appliance repairs)
- Health and safety concerns
- Disputes or conflicts

Having a plan in place ensures that everyone is prepared for various scenarios and can respond appropriately when needed.

12. Be Open to Negotiation:

Flexibility and a willingness to negotiate are key to successful shared living arrangements. While it's essential to have clear expectations and guidelines, be open to compromise and adjustments when necessary. Keep in mind that living with roommates often requires give-and-take to maintain a harmonious environment.

13. Review and Sign Agreements:

Once you've completed the screening process, conducted interviews, and discussed expectations, review all agreements with potential roommates. This includes the roommate agreement, rent division, and shared responsibilities. Ensure that everyone is comfortable with the terms before proceeding.

14. Keep Communication Open:

Open and respectful communication is the cornerstone of a successful living arrangement with roommates. Throughout your cohabitation, maintain regular communication to address any issues or changes in circumstances. Encourage roommates to voice concerns or suggestions openly and work together to find solutions.

15. Handle Conflicts Constructively:

Conflict is a natural part of shared living, but how you handle it can make all the difference. When conflicts arise, address them promptly and constructively. Refer to the roommate agreement and agreed-upon house rules to find solutions. Maintain a respectful and solution-oriented approach to maintain a harmonious living environment.

Chapter 4: Alternative Housing Options

Exploring Co-Living Spaces: Concept and How to Find Them

In recent years, co-living spaces have gained traction as a dynamic alternative to traditional housing arrangements, particularly in densely populated urban areas where housing costs are soaring. Co-living offers a distinctive blend of affordability, community, and convenience, making it an appealing option for a wide range of individuals. In this chapter, we will delve into the concept of co-living spaces, understand their advantages, and explore how to find them.

Understanding Co-Living Spaces:

Co-living spaces are more than just a housing solution; they represent a lifestyle and a philosophy that seeks to redefine modern living. Here are the key elements that characterize co-living spaces:

1. Shared Living Areas:

- At the heart of co-living spaces are shared living areas. These spaces are designed to encourage social interaction among residents. Typically, you'll find communal kitchens, common rooms, and dining spaces. This arrangement fosters a sense of togetherness and community, making co-living an attractive choice for those seeking connections in an increasingly digital world.

2. Private and Shared Bedrooms:

- Co-living spaces offer a blend of personal privacy and communal living. Residents typically have their private bedrooms, ensuring a level of solitude and personal space. For those looking to save even more on housing costs, some co-living spaces also offer shared bedrooms at a lower rate.

3. Fully Furnished Accommodations:

- One of the conveniences of co-living is that these spaces are often fully furnished. This eliminates the need to invest in furniture or undergo the hassle of moving bulky items. You can simply move in with your personal belongings and start enjoying your new living space.

4. Utilities and Services Included:

- Many co-living arrangements include utilities such as water, electricity, internet, and sometimes even cleaning services in the monthly rent. This all-inclusive approach simplifies budgeting and helps residents avoid unexpected financial burdens.

5. Community and Events:

- Co-living spaces place a strong emphasis on building a vibrant community. They organize events, activities, and shared experiences that bring residents together. These events can range from communal dinners and workshops to fitness classes and networking sessions. Such a focus on community enrichment often leads to valuable social connections and the opportunity to forge lasting friendships.

6. Flexibility and Short Leases:

- Unlike traditional long-term leases, co-living often offers flexible terms. You may find month-to-month options or short-term leases that cater to various lifestyles. This flexibility is particularly attractive to individuals who prefer to avoid lengthy commitments and desire the freedom to adapt to changing circumstances.

Why Co-Living?

Co-living spaces have gained prominence due to several compelling advantages:

1. Affordability: With rising housing costs in many urban areas, co-living provides a cost-effective solution. By sharing expenses like rent, utilities, and even groceries with other residents, individuals can significantly reduce their monthly housing expenditures. This affordability factor is especially appealing to young professionals, students, and those looking to save for future financial goals.

2. Community and Social Connection: In an age of digital isolation, co-living spaces offer a respite. They provide an environment where forming meaningful connections with fellow residents is not just encouraged but woven into the fabric of daily life. The shared living areas, communal events, and collaborative atmosphere foster a sense of belonging and social interaction that can be rare in traditional housing.

3. Convenience and Fully Equipped Spaces: Co-living eliminates the hassles of furniture shopping and setting up utilities. Residents can move into a fully furnished space with all essential amenities already in place. This convenience makes co-living an attractive choice, especially for those relocating to a new city or country.

4. Flexibility and Reduced Commitment: Traditional leases often require long-term commitments that can be burdensome. Co-living spaces provide the flexibility to adapt to changing circumstances. Whether you're planning a short stay in a city or simply prefer not to be tied down by a lengthy lease, co-living offers the freedom to tailor your housing arrangement to your needs.

How to Find Co-Living Spaces:

Now that you understand the concept and advantages of co-living, let's explore how to find these innovative housing options:

1. Online Platforms:

- Begin your search by exploring online platforms that specialize in co-living listings. Websites like CoLiving.com, Common, Roam, and several others offer comprehensive databases of co-living spaces available in different locations. These platforms typically provide detailed information about each space, including photos, pricing, amenities, and resident reviews.

2. Local Listings:

- Don't limit your search to online platforms alone. Check local classified ads, community bulletin boards, and real estate listings in your desired area. Smaller co-living communities may not be listed on larger platforms, so local listings can sometimes yield hidden gems.

3. Social Media and Groups:

- Social media platforms and online communities related to housing or co-living can be valuable resources. Join relevant groups or follow accounts that share co-living listings and updates. Engaging with these communities can provide access to firsthand recommendations and insights.

4. Co-Living Companies:

- Explore co-living companies that operate in your desired city or region. These companies specialize in creating and managing co-living spaces, and they often have multiple locations to choose from. Research their offerings, visit their websites, and reach out for availability and pricing.

5. Attend Co-Living Events:

- Some cities host co-living events or open houses where you can physically visit co-living spaces, meet current residents, and learn more about the communities. Attending such events provides a firsthand look at what each space has to offer and allows you to ask questions and gather information.

6. Specify Your Preferences:

- To narrow down your search effectively, be specific about your preferences. Consider factors such as location, budget, desired amenities, and the type of community you'd like to join. The more specific you are, the easier it will be to find a co-living space that suits your needs.

7. Visit and Tour:

- Before committing to a co-living space, schedule visits and tours. This step is crucial to gaining a firsthand understanding of the environment, meeting potential roommates or community members, and evaluating the overall atmosphere. It's also an opportunity to ask questions and address any concerns.

8. Review Agreements and Terms:

- Carefully review the co-living agreement or lease terms. Understand the rent structure, included services, and any house rules or community guidelines. This documentation outlines the expectations and commitments of both residents and the co-living management.

9. Connect with Current Residents:

- Whenever possible, try to connect with current residents or members of the co-living community. These individuals can provide invaluable insights into daily life within the space, the atmosphere, and what to expect as a resident.

10. Consider Commute and Location: - Evaluate the proximity of the co-living space to your workplace, public transportation, and essential amenities. A convenient location can significantly impact your daily life and reduce commuting stress.

11. Budget and Affordability: - Ensure that the co-living arrangement aligns with your budget and financial goals. Calculate the overall monthly cost, including rent, utilities, and any additional fees. Compare this to your budget to ensure a comfortable fit.

12. Compatibility and Community: - Reflect on whether the co-living community's values, lifestyle, and culture align with your own. Compatibility with your potential roommates and neighbors is essential for a positive and fulfilling co-living experience.

13. Legal Considerations: - Familiarize yourself with local tenant rights and regulations that apply to co-living arrangements. Ensure that the co-living space complies with all legal requirements to protect your rights as a resident.

14. Review the Contract: - Before finalizing your decision, carefully review the co-living contract or lease agreement. Pay attention to termination clauses, security deposits, and any penalties for breaking the lease. Understanding the terms and conditions is crucial for a smooth living experience.

15. Make an Informed Decision: - After conducting thorough research, visiting potential co-living spaces, and considering all relevant factors, make an informed decision that aligns with your lifestyle and objectives.

Benefits of Tiny Homes and Micro-Apartments:

Tiny homes and micro-apartments are part of a growing movement that challenges the conventional idea that more space equates to a higher quality of life. These smaller living spaces offer several advantages:

1. **Affordability:** Both tiny homes and micro-apartments tend to be more affordable than larger homes or apartments. The lower upfront cost and reduced ongoing expenses, such as utility bills and maintenance, can significantly decrease the financial burden on residents.
2. **Sustainability:** Smaller living spaces are inherently more sustainable. They require fewer building materials, consume less energy, and have a smaller environmental footprint. This appeals to individuals who prioritize eco-friendly living and reducing their carbon footprint.
3. **Minimalist Lifestyle:** Living in a smaller space encourages a

minimalist lifestyle. Residents must prioritize their possessions, which can lead to reduced clutter and a simpler, more organized life. This shift towards minimalism can result in reduced stress and a greater focus on experiences over material possessions.

4. **Location and Accessibility:** Many tiny homes and micro-apartments are strategically located in urban centers or desirable areas, making them accessible to workplaces, amenities, and public transportation. This can lead to a more convenient and efficient daily life, reducing commuting time and expenses.
5. **Lower Utility Costs:** Smaller living spaces require less energy for heating, cooling, and lighting, leading to lower utility bills. This cost savings can contribute to improved financial stability.

Challenges of Tiny Homes and Micro-Apartments:

While tiny homes and micro-apartments offer numerous benefits, they also present certain challenges:

1. **Limited Space:** The most apparent challenge is the limited living space. This may require residents to adapt their lifestyles significantly, including downsizing belongings and reevaluating their spatial needs.
2. **Storage Constraints:** With less square footage, storage space is at a premium. Finding creative and efficient storage solutions is essential to maintain a clutter-free and functional living environment.
3. **Privacy Concerns:** Tiny homes and micro-apartments may not provide the same level of privacy as larger living spaces. Communal facilities or shared walls may result in noise disturbances or a lack of personal space.
4. **Zoning and Regulation Issues:** In some areas, zoning regulations and building codes may pose challenges for those interested in tiny homes. Certain municipalities may have minimum square footage requirements for dwellings or restrictions on where tiny homes can be placed.
5. **Limited Resale Value:** Smaller living spaces may have limited resale value compared to traditional homes. Potential buyers may have

reservations about the size and layout, which can affect the resale price and marketability.

6. **Adaptation and Lifestyle Adjustment:** Transitioning to a tiny home or micro-apartment often requires a significant lifestyle adjustment. Individuals must be prepared to embrace a simpler, more compact way of living.
7. **Accessibility and Aging:** Tiny homes and micro-apartments may not be suitable for individuals with mobility issues or those who anticipate needing more space in the future. Aging in place in such small spaces can be challenging.
8. **Legal and Regulatory Hurdles:** Navigating legal and regulatory aspects, such as property zoning, building codes, and land use regulations, can be complex when it comes to tiny homes. Residents may face legal hurdles depending on their location and the type of tiny home they choose.

Understanding House Hacking:

House hacking involves purchasing a property with the intention of living in it while simultaneously renting out a portion of the property to generate rental income. The goal is to offset or even fully cover your own housing expenses, making homeownership more affordable and potentially profitable.

Benefits of House Hacking:

1. **Reduced Housing Costs:** House hacking allows you to significantly reduce or eliminate your own housing expenses. By renting out a portion of your property, you can use the rental income to cover your mortgage, property taxes, insurance, and maintenance costs.
2. **Build Wealth:** House hacking can be a wealth-building strategy. As you collect rental income and your property's value appreciates over time, you can build equity and wealth through real estate ownership.
3. **Lower Down Payment:** Depending on the type of property and your qualifications, you may be able to purchase a house-hacking property with a lower down payment, making homeownership more accessible.

4. **Tax Benefits:** Rental income can have tax advantages, including deductions for mortgage interest, property taxes, and certain expenses related to maintaining the rental portion of your property.
5. **Real Estate Experience:** House hacking provides an opportunity to gain experience as a landlord and property manager. This experience can be valuable if you plan to invest in additional rental properties in the future.
6. **Flexible Living Arrangements:** House hacking doesn't restrict you to a particular property type. You can choose a single-family home with a separate rental unit, a multi-unit property (like a duplex or triplex), or even a spare room in your current residence.

How to Implement House Hacking Successfully:

Implementing a successful house hacking strategy involves careful planning and execution. Here's a step-by-step guide to get you started:

1. Define Your Goals:

- Determine your financial goals and what you aim to achieve through house hacking. Are you looking to eliminate your housing expenses, build wealth, or both? Having clear objectives will guide your strategy.

2. Budget and Financing:

- Assess your financial situation and establish a budget for your house hacking property. Consider your down payment, monthly mortgage payment, property taxes, insurance, and maintenance costs. Explore mortgage options tailored to house hacking, such as FHA loans for multi-unit properties.

3. Choose the Right Property:

- Select a property that suits your goals and budget. Look for homes with a layout that allows for rental separation, whether it's a separate unit, a finished basement, or a spare room with a private entrance.

4. Run the Numbers:

- Calculate potential rental income based on market rents in your area. Ensure that the rental income covers your housing expenses and leaves room for profit. Consider the costs of property management, maintenance, and vacancies.

5. Legal and Zoning Considerations:

- Familiarize yourself with local laws, zoning regulations, and homeowner association rules related to house hacking. Ensure that your property and intended rental arrangement comply with these regulations.

6. Tenant Selection:

- Be selective when choosing tenants for your rental unit. Screen applicants carefully, checking references, conducting background checks, and evaluating their ability to pay rent consistently.

7. Property Management:

- Decide whether you will manage the property yourself or hire a property management company. Managing the property yourself can save money, but it also requires time and effort.

8. Lease Agreements:

- Draft comprehensive lease agreements that outline the terms and responsibilities of both you and your tenants. Clearly define rent, security deposits, maintenance responsibilities, and other important details.

9. Maintenance and Repairs:

- Keep the property well-maintained to attract and retain quality tenants. Address repairs and maintenance promptly to ensure the property remains in good condition.

10. Financial Management: - Maintain a separate bank account for rental income and expenses. Keep thorough financial records for tax purposes and budgeting.

11. Be a Responsive Landlord: - Foster a positive landlord-tenant relationship by being responsive to tenant needs and concerns. Promptly address any issues or maintenance requests.

12. Evaluate and Optimize: - Periodically evaluate your house hacking strategy to ensure it aligns with your goals. Consider refinancing opportunities, property improvements, or adjustments to rent rates if necessary.

House hacking can be a powerful way to reduce housing expenses, build wealth, and gain valuable real estate experience. By carefully planning, selecting the right property, and effectively managing your rental unit, you can make the most of this strategy and achieve your financial objectives.

The Nomadic Lifestyle:

RV and van living represent a lifestyle of mobility, adventure, and simplicity. Individuals who embrace this way of life often prioritize experiences and exploration over material possessions. Here are some key elements of the nomadic lifestyle:

1. **Freedom of Mobility:** RV and van dwellers have the freedom to travel and explore new places continuously. They can wake up to breathtaking landscapes, change their scenery whenever they please, and live life on the open road.
2. **Minimalist Living:** Living in a confined space requires downsizing possessions to the essentials. This minimalist approach can lead to a simplified and clutter-free life.
3. **Connection with Nature:** RV and van living often involve spending time in natural settings, such as national parks, beaches, and forests.

This close connection with nature can lead to a greater appreciation for the environment.

4. **Community:** There is a thriving community of RV and van dwellers who connect through social media, forums, and in person at various gatherings and events. This sense of community provides support, camaraderie, and shared experiences.

Financial Aspects of RV and Van Living:

While RV and van living offer a unique lifestyle, they also come with financial considerations that differ from traditional housing. Here's a closer look at the financial aspects:

1. Lower Housing Costs:

- RV and van living can significantly reduce housing costs. While there are upfront expenses for purchasing an RV or van and outfitting it for living, ongoing housing expenses such as rent or a mortgage are often eliminated. Campsite fees, fuel, and maintenance costs become the primary housing expenses.

2. Flexibility and Adaptability:

- The nomadic lifestyle allows for flexibility in choosing where to stay. RV and van dwellers can opt for free or low-cost camping options in national forests, Bureau of Land Management (BLM) land, or public lands. Additionally, they can choose to stay in campgrounds with varying amenities and costs.

3. Reduced Utilities:

- RVs and vans are designed for self-sufficiency. They often include water tanks, solar panels, and energy-efficient appliances. As a result, utility costs are typically lower, and in some cases, can be eliminated entirely by harnessing solar power.

4. Minimal Possessions:

- Living in a small space encourages minimalism. With limited room for belongings, individuals tend to spend less on material possessions, leading to potential cost savings.

5. Budgeting and Expense Tracking:

- Successful RV and van living requires meticulous budgeting and expense tracking. Nomadic individuals must plan for fuel, maintenance, groceries, and other travel-related costs. Tools and apps can help with budgeting and financial management.

6. Income Sources:

- Many RV and van dwellers work remotely, enabling them to maintain a steady income while traveling. Others rely on seasonal or temporary work opportunities in the locations they visit. Some individuals have passive income sources, such as investments or online businesses.

7. Healthcare Considerations:

- Healthcare is a critical aspect of RV and van living. Nomadic individuals must consider health insurance, access to medical care on the road, and emergency planning. Health savings accounts (HSAs) and telemedicine services can be valuable resources.

8. Emergency Fund:

- Maintaining a robust emergency fund is essential for handling unexpected expenses, such as vehicle repairs or medical emergencies, while living a nomadic lifestyle. An emergency fund provides financial security and peace of mind.

9. Legal and Regulatory Considerations:

- RV and van dwellers must navigate a variety of legal and regulatory issues, including vehicle registration, driver's licenses, and residency requirements. Familiarity with these requirements is essential to avoid legal complications.

10. Environmental Responsibility: - RV and van dwellers often embrace sustainable practices, such as reducing waste, conserving water and energy, and respecting the environment. These practices can lead to cost savings and a reduced ecological footprint.

Homesteading and Rural Living: Affordable Housing with Self-Sufficiency

Homesteading and rural living are alternative housing options that offer a unique blend of affordability, self-sufficiency, and a deep connection to nature. In this section, we'll delve into these alternatives, exploring their affordability and the compelling benefits they provide.

Homesteading Defined:

Homesteading is a lifestyle rooted in self-sufficiency and sustainability. It typically involves living on a piece of rural or semi-rural land and producing a significant portion of one's own food, energy, and other necessities. Here are key aspects of homesteading:

1. **Self-Reliance:** Homesteaders aim to reduce their dependence on external resources. They often grow their own fruits and vegetables, raise livestock, and harness renewable energy sources like solar or wind power.
2. **Sustainable Practices:** Sustainability is a core principle of homesteading. Homesteaders prioritize practices such as composting, rainwater harvesting, and organic gardening to minimize their environmental impact.
3. **Reduced Expenses:** By producing their own food and energy, homesteaders can significantly reduce their monthly expenses. This financial independence aligns with the goal of affordable living.
4. **Skills Development:** Homesteading fosters a diverse skill set,

including gardening, animal husbandry, food preservation, and DIY home improvement. These skills can lead to cost savings and self-sufficiency.

Rural Living in General:

Rural living encompasses a wide range of lifestyles in rural or semi-rural areas. It may or may not involve full-fledged homesteading practices. Here are some aspects of rural living:

1. **Lower Cost of Living:** Rural areas often have a lower cost of living compared to urban centers. This includes lower housing costs, property taxes, and utility expenses.
2. **Natural Beauty:** Rural living provides access to natural landscapes, clean air, and a slower pace of life. This can contribute to improved well-being and reduced stress.
3. **Community Bonds:** Rural communities often have strong social ties, fostering a sense of belonging and support among residents.
4. **Varied Housing Options:** Rural areas offer diverse housing options, from traditional single-family homes to farms, ranches, and small cottages. This diversity can cater to various preferences and budgets.

The Affordability of Homesteading and Rural Living:

1. **Reduced Housing Costs:** Homesteading often involves purchasing rural land at a lower cost than urban real estate. Building a home on this land can be more affordable than buying an existing urban property.
2. **Lower Property Taxes:** Rural areas typically have lower property tax rates than urban areas. This contributes to ongoing cost savings for homeowners.
3. **Self-Sufficiency Savings:** By producing their own food and energy, homesteaders can significantly reduce grocery bills and utility expenses.
4. **Minimalist Lifestyle:** Both homesteading and rural living encourage

a minimalist mindset, where individuals prioritize needs over wants. This can lead to reduced spending on material possessions.

5. **Resourceful Living:** Living in rural areas often encourages resourcefulness. Residents learn to repair, repurpose, and make the most of available resources, which can lead to cost savings.

Challenges to Consider:

1. **Infrastructure and Services:** Rural areas may have limited access to healthcare, education, and other essential services. This should be factored into your decision.
2. **Distance to Work:** Commuting to urban job centers may be necessary for some rural residents, potentially offsetting the cost savings of rural living.
3. **Learning Curve:** Homesteading and rural living require learning new skills and adapting to a different way of life. There can be a steep learning curve for those new to these lifestyles.

In summary, homesteading and rural living offer affordable housing alternatives that emphasize self-sufficiency, sustainability, and a close connection to nature. These lifestyles can lead to reduced housing costs, lower property taxes, and savings through self-sufficiency. However, they come with challenges related to access to services and potential commuting distances. For individuals seeking a simpler, more affordable way of life that aligns with environmental stewardship and self-reliance, homesteading and rural living are compelling options to explore.

Chapter 5: Passive Income Streams

Explaining Passive Income and Its Role in Offseting Housing Costs

Passive income is a financial concept that plays a crucial role in reducing housing costs and achieving greater financial independence. In this chapter, we will delve into the concept of passive income, its significance, and how it can be leveraged to offset housing expenses effectively.

Understanding Passive Income:

Passive income is money earned with minimal effort or direct involvement. It is income that flows in regularly with little ongoing effort once the initial work or investment is made. Passive income can be generated from various sources, including investments, real estate, royalties, and business ventures. The key characteristic of passive income is that it requires less active participation compared to earned income, such as a traditional job where you exchange time for money.

Sources of Passive Income:

1. **Investments:** Investments like stocks, bonds, mutual funds, and dividend-paying assets can generate passive income in the form of interest, dividends, or capital gains. These investments provide income without the need for daily management.
2. **Real Estate:** Real estate investments, such as rental properties, can generate passive income through monthly rent payments. Real estate investment trusts (REITs) and real estate crowdfunding platforms also offer opportunities for passive income from real estate.
3. **Royalties:** Authors, musicians, artists, and inventors can earn royalties from their creative works or intellectual property. These payments can provide ongoing income for years.
4. **Business Ownership:** Passive income can be derived from owning a share of a business or participating in a profitable business venture where your involvement is limited, such as being a silent partner.
5. **Dividend Stocks:** Some stocks pay regular dividends to

shareholders. These dividends can provide a consistent source of passive income.

The Role of Passive Income in Offseting Housing Costs:

Passive income plays a significant role in offsetting housing costs by providing an additional source of income that can be directed toward mortgage payments, rent, property taxes, and other housing-related expenses. Here's how passive income can help in this regard:

1. **Financial Flexibility:** Passive income provides financial flexibility, allowing individuals to allocate a portion of their earnings specifically to cover housing costs. This reduces the burden on their primary income source.
2. **Debt Reduction:** For homeowners with mortgages, passive income can be directed toward paying down the principal balance of the loan. Accelerated mortgage payments can lead to significant interest savings over time.
3. **Rental Income:** Individuals who invest in rental properties can use rental income to offset their own housing costs. This can lead to a situation where rental income covers or even exceeds the expenses of the property, providing additional income.
4. **Investment Diversification:** Passive income diversifies income streams, reducing reliance on a single source of income, such as a job. This diversification can enhance financial stability and resilience in the face of economic uncertainties.
5. **Long-Term Financial Goals:** Passive income contributes to achieving long-term financial goals, such as saving for retirement or building wealth. By using passive income to cover housing expenses, individuals free up more of their primary income to invest and grow their wealth.
6. **Enhanced Financial Security:** Passive income creates a safety net, ensuring that individuals have a consistent flow of funds to cover essential expenses, including housing costs, even during periods of economic downturns or unexpected financial challenges.

Generating Passive Income for Housing Costs:

To generate passive income for housing costs, individuals can explore various strategies based on their financial goals, risk tolerance, and available resources. Here are some common approaches:

1. **Investing in Dividend Stocks:** Investing in dividend-paying stocks can provide regular dividend income that can be directed toward housing expenses.
2. **Real Estate Investments:** Owning rental properties or participating in real estate investment opportunities, such as REITs, can generate rental income that offsets housing costs.
3. **Investment Portfolios:** Diversified investment portfolios that include income-generating assets can yield regular returns that contribute to housing expenses.
4. **Side Businesses:** Establishing a side business or venture that requires limited ongoing involvement can generate additional income to cover housing costs.
5. **Royalties and Intellectual Property:** For those with creative talents or intellectual property, monetizing their work through royalties or licensing agreements can provide passive income.
6. **Peer-to-Peer Lending and Crowdfunding:** Participating in peer-to-peer lending platforms or crowdfunding projects can yield interest or dividend income that can be used for housing expenses.

Real Estate Investments: Rental Properties and Real Estate Investment Trusts (REITs)

Real estate investments are a well-established avenue for generating passive income. In this section, we'll explore two prominent forms of real estate investments: rental properties and Real Estate Investment Trusts (REITs). These investment options offer opportunities for individuals to earn rental income and dividends without active day-to-day involvement in property management.

Rental Properties: A Hands-On Investment

Rental properties involve purchasing residential or commercial real estate with the intention of generating rental income. Here's an overview of how rental properties work and their role in passive income generation:

1. Property Acquisition: Investors purchase one or more properties with the goal of renting them out to tenants. These properties can range from single-family homes and apartments to commercial spaces.

2. Rental Income: The primary source of passive income from rental properties is the monthly rent collected from tenants. This income can help offset the property's expenses, including mortgage payments, property taxes, insurance, and maintenance costs.

3. Property Management: While rental income can be passive, property management can be a more hands-on aspect of owning rental properties. Investors can choose to manage the properties themselves or hire property management companies to handle day-to-day operations, such as tenant screening, maintenance, and rent collection.

4. Equity Building: Over time, rental property owners build equity in their properties as they pay down mortgages. Additionally, properties may appreciate in value, potentially leading to capital gains upon sale.

5. Tax Benefits: Rental property owners can take advantage of various tax deductions, such as mortgage interest, property taxes, and depreciation, which can reduce their overall tax liability.

Real Estate Investment Trusts (REITs): A Passive Investment Vehicle

Real Estate Investment Trusts (REITs) are a passive investment option that allows individuals to invest in a diversified portfolio of income-producing real estate assets. Here's an overview of REITs and how they contribute to passive income:

1. Investment in Real Estate Securities: REITs are companies or trusts that own and manage income-generating real estate properties, such as office buildings, shopping centers, apartment complexes, and hotels. Investors can buy shares in these REITs, which are traded on stock exchanges.

2. Dividend Income: REITs are required by law to distribute at least 90% of their taxable income to shareholders in the form of dividends. As a result, investors in REITs typically receive regular dividend payments, which can serve as a source of passive income.

3. Diversification: REITs provide investors with exposure to a diverse range of real estate assets without the need to buy and manage properties individually. This diversification can reduce risk and enhance income stability.

4. Liquidity: Unlike direct ownership of rental properties, which can be less liquid, REIT shares can be bought and sold easily on stock exchanges, offering investors greater liquidity.

5. Professional Management: REITs are managed by real estate professionals who handle property acquisition, leasing, management, and maintenance. This relieves investors of the responsibilities associated with direct property ownership.

6. Accessibility: REITs make real estate investing accessible to a broader range of investors, including those with smaller budgets who may not have the means to purchase physical properties.

Choosing Between Rental Properties and REITs:

The choice between investing in rental properties and REITs depends on individual preferences, financial goals, and risk tolerance. Rental properties offer direct ownership and potential for higher returns but require more active involvement in property management. REITs, on the other hand, provide passive income with professional management and diversification.

Investors should consider their financial situation, investment horizon, and level of involvement they are comfortable with when deciding between these two real estate investment options. Some individuals may even choose to include both rental properties and REITs in their investment portfolio to achieve a balanced approach to real estate investing.

Introducing Dividend Stocks: A Steady Income Stream

Dividend stocks are a prominent form of passive income investment, known for their ability to provide a reliable and consistent income stream to investors. In this section, we will introduce the concept of dividend stocks and explain how they can play a vital role in generating steady passive income.

Understanding Dividend Stocks:

Dividend stocks represent shares of publicly traded companies that have a history of distributing a portion of their earnings to shareholders in the form of dividends. These dividends are typically paid on a regular basis, often quarterly, and are usually expressed as a fixed amount per share or as a percentage of the stock's current price, known as the dividend yield.

How Dividend Stocks Work:

Here's a simplified overview of how dividend stocks work:

1. **Stock Ownership:** Investors purchase shares of a dividend-paying company's stock. Each share represents ownership in the company.
2. **Dividend Declaration:** The company's board of directors declares a dividend, specifying the amount to be paid per share. This decision is typically based on the company's financial performance, profitability, and cash flow.
3. **Payment Frequency:** Dividends are typically paid on a regular schedule, such as quarterly, although some companies may pay them monthly or annually.
4. **Distribution:** On the specified payment date, shareholders receive their dividend payments directly into their brokerage accounts or through physical checks, depending on their preference and the brokerage's policies.

The Role of Dividend Stocks in Generating Passive Income:

Dividend stocks serve as a powerful tool for generating passive income due to several key characteristics:

1. **Regular Income:** Dividend stocks provide a consistent income

stream. Shareholders can rely on these payments as a predictable source of passive income.

2. **Income Stability:** Established dividend-paying companies tend to maintain stable dividend payments, even during economic downturns. This income stability can provide financial security.
3. **Income Growth:** Many dividend-paying companies increase their dividends over time as their earnings grow. This results in rising income for shareholders, helping to offset the effects of inflation.
4. **Portfolio Diversification:** Including dividend stocks in an investment portfolio can enhance diversification, as these stocks often come from various sectors of the economy.
5. **Long-Term Wealth Building:** Reinvesting dividend income by purchasing more shares (a strategy known as dividend reinvestment) can accelerate the growth of an investment portfolio, leading to greater wealth over time.

Types of Dividend Stocks:

Dividend stocks can be categorized based on the nature of their dividend payments:

1. **Dividend Aristocrats:** These are companies that have a history of consistently increasing their dividends for at least 25 consecutive years. They are known for their commitment to rewarding shareholders.
2. **High-Yield Dividend Stocks:** These stocks offer higher dividend yields but may have slower dividend growth. They are favored by income-focused investors seeking immediate cash flow.
3. **Growth Dividend Stocks:** These companies prioritize reinvesting profits for growth but still offer dividends. They are often associated with younger, high-growth companies.

Considerations for Dividend Stock Investing:

Investing in dividend stocks requires careful consideration of individual financial goals and risk tolerance. Here are some factors to keep in mind:

1. **Diversification:** Diversify your dividend stock holdings across different sectors and industries to reduce risk.
2. **Dividend Yield:** Consider the yield offered by a stock, but also assess the company's financial health and ability to maintain dividends.
3. **Dividend History:** Research a company's dividend history, including its track record of dividend increases and consistency.
4. **Risk Tolerance:** Be aware that the stock market can be volatile, and stock prices can fluctuate. Assess your risk tolerance and investment horizon.
5. **Tax Implications:** Dividend income may be subject to different tax rates, so it's essential to understand the tax implications of your investments.

Exploring Peer-to-Peer Lending: Generating Passive Income Through Lending Platforms

Peer-to-peer (P2P) lending platforms represent a modern and innovative way to generate passive income by connecting investors with borrowers. In this section, we will explore P2P lending platforms, their potential for passive income, and how you can participate in this lending model.

Understanding Peer-to-Peer Lending:

Peer-to-peer lending, often referred to as P2P lending or marketplace lending, is a financial model that enables individuals to lend money directly to other individuals or small businesses through online platforms. These platforms act as intermediaries, facilitating loan origination, servicing, and repayment. P2P lending differs from traditional bank lending in that it connects individual lenders (investors) with borrowers, cutting out traditional financial institutions.

How Peer-to-Peer Lending Works:

Here's an overview of how P2P lending works:

1. **Investor Registration:** Individuals interested in participating in P2P lending register as investors on P2P lending platforms.

2. **Borrower Application:** Borrowers apply for loans by submitting their loan requests and financial information through the platform.
3. **Risk Assessment:** P2P lending platforms typically assess borrower creditworthiness and assign risk ratings to loan listings.
4. **Loan Listings:** Approved loan requests are listed on the platform, specifying the loan amount, interest rate, and loan term.
5. **Investor Selection:** Investors review available loan listings and choose which loans to fund based on their risk tolerance and investment preferences.
6. **Funding:** When enough investors commit to funding a loan listing, the loan is fully funded, and the borrower receives the requested funds.
7. **Loan Repayment:** Borrowers make regular monthly payments, which include both principal and interest. These payments are distributed to investors.

The Potential for Passive Income:

P2P lending platforms offer investors the opportunity to earn passive income through interest payments on the loans they fund. Here's how P2P lending can be a source of passive income:

1. **Regular Interest Payments:** Investors receive monthly interest payments from borrowers, providing a consistent stream of income.
2. **Diversification:** To manage risk, investors can diversify their investments across multiple loans, spreading their exposure.
3. **Reinvestment:** As borrowers make payments, investors can reinvest those funds into new loans, compounding their returns.
4. **Loan Origination and Servicing:** P2P lending platforms handle loan origination, servicing, and collections, minimizing the effort required from investors.

Practical Advice for Managing and Diversifying Passive Income Sources:

Managing and diversifying passive income sources is essential for financial stability and long-term success. Here are some practical strategies:

1. **Diversify Your Portfolio:** Avoid putting all your passive income eggs in one basket. Diversify across various asset classes, such as dividend stocks, rental properties, and P2P lending.
2. **Risk Assessment:** Assess the risk associated with each passive income source. Consider factors like liquidity, volatility, and the potential for income interruptions.
3. **Invest for the Long Term:** Many passive income sources, such as dividend stocks and real estate, benefit from a long-term investment horizon. Patience can lead to compounding growth.
4. **Reinvest Earnings:** Whenever possible, reinvest passive income earnings to accelerate your portfolio's growth.
5. **Tax Planning:** Be mindful of the tax implications of your passive income sources. Some investments may offer tax advantages or require specific tax strategies.
6. **Regular Review:** Periodically review your passive income sources and overall financial strategy. Make adjustments as needed to align with your goals and changing circumstances.
7. **Emergency Fund:** Maintain an emergency fund to cover unexpected expenses, ensuring that your passive income sources remain intact.
8. **Professional Advice:** Consider consulting with a financial advisor or tax professional to optimize your passive income strategy and tax efficiency.
9. **Lifestyle Considerations:** Passive income sources can contribute to your desired lifestyle. Consider how your passive income aligns with your financial goals and lifestyle choices.

Chapter 6: Homeownership Strategies

Tips for DIY Home Maintenance and Repair

Owning a home comes with the responsibility of maintaining and occasionally repairing various aspects of the property. While some maintenance tasks and repairs may require professional help, there are several DIY (Do-It-Yourself) home maintenance and repair tasks that homeowners can tackle to save on maintenance costs. In this section, we'll provide tips and guidance for these tasks.

1. Regular Home Inspections:

One of the best ways to catch maintenance issues early is by conducting regular home inspections. This involves visually inspecting different areas of your home, such as the roof, plumbing, electrical systems, and foundation, to identify any signs of wear, damage, or potential problems. Regular inspections can help you address issues before they become major repairs.

2. Learn Basic Plumbing Skills:

Knowing how to handle minor plumbing issues can save you a significant amount on repair costs. Learn how to fix leaky faucets, replace washers, and unclog drains. Having some plumbing tools, like a plunger and pipe wrench, can be beneficial for these tasks.

3. Electrical Maintenance:

For basic electrical maintenance, you can replace light switches, electrical outlets, and light fixtures. Make sure to turn off the power to the area you're working on to ensure safety. However, for more complex electrical issues, it's crucial to hire a licensed electrician.

4. Painting and Drywall Repair:

Painting your home's interior or exterior is a common DIY project that can refresh the appearance of your property. Additionally, you can learn how to patch small holes and cracks in drywall to maintain the integrity of your walls.

5. Roof and Gutter Maintenance:

Regularly inspect your roof for loose or damaged shingles. Replace damaged shingles promptly to prevent water leaks. Keep gutters clean and free of debris to ensure proper drainage and prevent water damage to your home's foundation.

6. Landscaping and Yard Maintenance:

Maintaining your landscaping and yard can improve your home's curb appeal and prevent potential issues. Regularly trim trees and shrubs away from the house to prevent damage to siding and roofs. Proper lawn care can also contribute to the overall health of your property.

7. HVAC System Maintenance:

While some HVAC maintenance tasks are best left to professionals, homeowners can change air filters regularly, clean vents and ducts, and ensure that outdoor AC units are free of debris to help maintain the efficiency of the system.

8. Small Appliance Repairs:

Basic troubleshooting and repairs of small appliances can save you money on replacement costs. Learn how to fix simple issues like a malfunctioning toaster or a leaking coffee maker.

9. Insulation and Weatherproofing:

Proper insulation and weatherproofing can improve energy efficiency. Learn how to seal gaps around windows and doors and add insulation where needed. This can result in lower heating and cooling costs.

10. Basic Carpentry Skills:

Basic carpentry skills can be handy for repairing or building simple structures around your home. For example, you can build shelves, repair wooden fences, or construct garden beds.

Safety Precautions for DIY Home Maintenance and Repair:

While DIY home maintenance and repairs can be cost-effective, safety should always be a top priority. Here are some safety precautions to keep in mind:

- **Use the Right Tools:** Make sure you have the necessary tools and equipment for each task, and use them correctly.
- **Educate Yourself:** Before attempting a DIY project, thoroughly research and understand the process. There are countless tutorials and guides available online.
- **Wear Appropriate Safety Gear:** Depending on the task, wear safety gear such as gloves, safety glasses, or a dust mask to protect yourself.
- **Turn Off Utilities:** When working on plumbing or electrical tasks, turn off the water supply or electricity to the area you're working on.
- **Know Your Limits:** If a project is beyond your skill level or poses safety risks, don't hesitate to seek professional help.

Your Feedback Matters:

We hope you find these DIY home maintenance and repair tips valuable in managing your home and saving on maintenance costs. Your feedback and experiences are important to us. If you've implemented any of these strategies or have additional insights to share, please consider writing a review or reaching out to us. Your input can help us continue to provide useful and practical advice to homeowners like you.

Exploring Home Sharing and Co-Ownership: Reducing Homeownership Expenses

Owning a home is a significant financial commitment, but there are innovative strategies that can help reduce homeownership expenses. In this section, we'll explore the benefits of home sharing and co-ownership as effective strategies to make homeownership more affordable.

Home Sharing: A Collaborative Approach

Home sharing involves individuals or families sharing a single residence, whether it's a house or an apartment. This approach offers several financial advantages:

1. Shared Mortgage Costs: By sharing the mortgage with another party, you can significantly reduce your monthly housing expenses. This can make homeownership more accessible for those who might struggle with the financial burden of owning a home on their own.

2. Splitting Utility Bills: Home sharers can also divide utility bills, such as electricity, water, and internet, which further reduces living costs.

3. Maintenance and Repairs: Shared homeownership often includes shared responsibilities for home maintenance and repairs. This can be cost-effective, as it allows individuals to pool resources and share the workload.

4. Shared Amenities: Many home sharing arrangements involve sharing common areas and amenities, such as kitchens, living rooms, and laundry facilities. This reduces the need for duplicate appliances and furnishings.

5. Flexibility: Home sharing can offer flexibility in terms of lease agreements, allowing participants to adapt the arrangement to their changing needs or financial situations.

Co-Ownership: Joint Ownership for Affordability

Co-ownership involves purchasing a property with one or more individuals, such as family members, friends, or co-investors, and sharing both the financial responsibilities and benefits. Here are the advantages of co-ownership:

1. Shared Purchase Costs: Co-owners can combine their financial resources to make a substantial down payment, reducing the overall cost of the property and potentially avoiding the need for private mortgage insurance (PMI).

2. Lower Monthly Payments: Sharing the mortgage payment and other housing-related expenses leads to lower monthly housing costs for each co-owner.

3. Diversification: Co-ownership diversifies the investment, spreading risk among multiple parties. This can be especially beneficial in fluctuating housing markets.

4. Enhanced Buying Power: Co-owners may qualify for larger loans or more favorable mortgage terms due to their combined financial strength.

5. Shared Responsibilities: Co-owners can divide responsibilities for home maintenance, repairs, and property management, making homeownership more manageable.

Important Considerations:

While home sharing and co-ownership offer significant benefits, it's essential to address several critical considerations to ensure a successful arrangement:

1. Legal Agreements: Develop clear legal agreements that outline the rights and responsibilities of each party involved. These agreements should cover property ownership, financial contributions, decision-making processes, and dispute resolution mechanisms.

2. Communication: Open and transparent communication is vital for resolving conflicts and ensuring that all co-owners or home sharers are on the same page regarding expectations and responsibilities.

3. Exit Strategies: Create exit strategies in case one or more co-owners or home sharers want to sell their share or leave the arrangement. This ensures a smooth transition and prevents potential disputes.

4. Legal and Financial Advice: Seek legal and financial advice when entering into co-ownership or home sharing arrangements. Professionals can help you navigate the legal and financial aspects of these agreements.

Responsible Mortgage Management:

Regardless of whether you choose home sharing, co-ownership, or traditional homeownership, responsible mortgage management is crucial. Here are some key principles:

1. **Affordability:** Ensure that your mortgage is affordable, with monthly payments that fit comfortably within your budget. Avoid overextending yourself financially.

2. **Regular Payments:** Make timely mortgage payments to maintain a good credit history and avoid penalties.

3. **Emergency Fund:** Build and maintain an emergency fund to cover unexpected home repairs or temporary financial setbacks.

4. **Mortgage Refinancing:** Explore mortgage refinancing options when interest rates are favorable. Refinancing can potentially lower your monthly mortgage payment.

5. **Consult Professionals:** Seek advice from mortgage professionals, financial advisors, and legal experts to make informed decisions regarding your mortgage and homeownership.

Chapter 7: Community Resources and Support

Accessing Nonprofit Organizations for Housing Assistance and Financial Education

In this chapter, we will explore the valuable resources offered by nonprofit organizations that focus on providing housing assistance, financial education, and a range of support services. These organizations play a vital role in helping individuals and families achieve their housing goals and improve their financial stability.

Nonprofit Organizations: Champions of Housing Assistance

Nonprofit organizations dedicated to housing assistance are often at the forefront of addressing housing challenges in communities. They offer a wide range of services designed to support individuals and families in their quest for affordable and stable housing. Here are some key ways these organizations can help:

1. **Affordable Housing Programs:** Many nonprofits work to develop, manage, and maintain affordable housing units. These units are typically available at below-market rents, making housing more accessible to low- and moderate-income individuals and families.
2. **Housing Counseling:** Nonprofit housing counseling agencies provide one-on-one counseling sessions to help individuals navigate the complexities of the housing market. They offer guidance on homebuying, foreclosure prevention, and tenant rights.
3. **Financial Education:** Nonprofits often offer financial education programs that empower individuals with the knowledge and skills needed to manage their finances effectively. This includes budgeting, debt management, and savings strategies.
4. **Homebuyer Education:** For aspiring homeowners, nonprofit organizations offer homebuyer education courses that cover topics such as mortgage financing, down payment assistance programs, and

the homebuying process.

5. **Rental Assistance:** Some nonprofits provide rental assistance programs to help individuals and families struggling to make rent payments. These programs can provide temporary relief during financial hardship.
6. **Home Rehabilitation:** Nonprofits may offer home repair and rehabilitation programs to assist homeowners with essential repairs and improvements to maintain the safety and habitability of their homes.
7. **Tenant Advocacy:** Nonprofits often advocate for tenant rights and work to prevent unfair housing practices and discrimination.

Local Government Programs: Support from Your Community

In addition to nonprofit organizations, local governments offer various programs and initiatives to assist individuals and families with housing needs. These programs are designed to promote affordable homeownership and rental opportunities. Here are some examples:

1. **First-Time Homebuyer Programs:** Many local governments offer programs that provide financial assistance, down payment grants, or low-interest loans to first-time homebuyers. These programs aim to make homeownership more attainable.
2. **Rental Assistance:** Some municipalities administer rental assistance programs that provide subsidies to eligible renters, reducing their monthly housing costs.
3. **Affordable Housing Initiatives:** Local governments may implement policies and zoning regulations to encourage the development of affordable housing units within their communities.
4. **Property Tax Relief:** Certain areas offer property tax relief or exemptions to low-income homeowners, helping them manage their housing expenses.
5. **Emergency Housing Assistance:** In times of crisis, such as natural disasters or economic downturns, local governments may provide emergency housing assistance to affected residents.

6. **Tenant Protections:** Local governments often enact tenant protection laws and regulations to safeguard renters from unfair practices and ensure the habitability of rental properties.

Navigating Community Resources:

When seeking assistance from nonprofit organizations or local government programs, consider the following steps:

1. **Research:** Identify the nonprofit organizations and government programs in your area that offer the specific assistance you need.
2. **Contact:** Reach out to these organizations or government agencies to inquire about their services, eligibility criteria, and application processes.
3. **Attend Workshops:** Attend workshops, seminars, or informational sessions provided by nonprofits or local government agencies to learn more about housing and financial education.
4. **Seek Guidance:** If needed, seek guidance from housing counselors or financial educators affiliated with nonprofit organizations to help you navigate the resources available to you.
5. **Apply Early:** Many assistance programs have limited funding, so it's essential to apply as early as possible if you believe you qualify for assistance.
6. **Stay Informed:** Keep abreast of changes in housing laws, regulations, and available programs within your community.

In summary, nonprofit organizations and local government programs play crucial roles in supporting individuals and families with housing assistance, financial education, and other essential services. By accessing these resources, you can gain valuable knowledge, financial stability, and the opportunity to achieve your housing goals, whether you are a renter or aspiring homeowner.

Advantages of Housing Cooperatives: Shared Expenses and Decision-Making

Housing cooperatives, often referred to as co-ops, offer a unique and collaborative approach to homeownership and affordable housing. In this section, we will delve into the advantages of participating in housing cooperatives, highlighting the benefits of shared expenses and decision-making.

Understanding Housing Cooperatives:

Housing cooperatives are a form of shared housing where residents collectively own and manage the property. Instead of owning individual units, co-op members own shares in the cooperative corporation, which, in turn, owns and operates the entire property. This collective ownership structure forms the foundation of the cooperative's advantages.

Advantages of Housing Cooperatives:

1. **Shared Expenses:** One of the primary advantages of housing cooperatives is the significant reduction in individual housing costs. Here's how it works:

- **Lower Mortgage Payments:** Co-op members collectively secure a mortgage for the property, spreading the debt across multiple members. As a result, individual mortgage payments are typically lower compared to purchasing a traditional single-family home.
- **Reduced Maintenance and Repair Costs:** Maintenance and repair expenses are shared among co-op members. The cooperative typically maintains a reserve fund for such expenses, which helps prevent individual members from facing significant financial burdens when unexpected repairs arise.
- **Economies of Scale:** Cooperative purchasing power can lead to cost savings in areas such as utilities, insurance, and landscaping services, ultimately reducing monthly expenses.

1. **Democratic Decision-Making:** Housing cooperatives operate on democratic principles, with members having a say in the management and policies of the co-op. This collective decision-making allows residents to shape the community according to their needs and

priorities.

2. **Affordability:** Co-op ownership often represents a more affordable path to homeownership, making it accessible to individuals and families who may struggle to purchase a traditional home.
3. **Community and Social Support:** Living in a cooperative can foster a strong sense of community. Co-op members often develop close relationships with their neighbors, providing social support and a sense of belonging.
4. **Stability and Long-Term Tenure:** Cooperative housing tends to provide stability and long-term tenure. Co-op members have a vested interest in the property's success and typically enjoy secure housing as long as they adhere to the cooperative's rules and responsibilities.

Stories of Affordable Housing Success:

Real-life stories often illustrate the transformative power of housing cooperatives and community support. Here are a couple of inspiring examples:

1. **Jane's Journey to Homeownership:**

Jane, a single mother of two, dreamed of owning a home but struggled to save for a down payment. She discovered a housing cooperative in her community that offered an affordable path to homeownership. By pooling resources with other co-op members, Jane was able to secure a mortgage and become a homeowner. The cooperative's supportive community allowed her to thrive as a homeowner and provide stability for her family.

1. **David's Cooperative Living Experience:**

David, a retiree on a fixed income, found the cost of maintaining his single-family home overwhelming. He decided to join a housing cooperative, attracted by the promise of shared expenses and a close-knit community. David's cooperative not only reduced his monthly housing costs but also provided a sense of belonging and companionship in his retirement years.

Taking Advantage of Community Resources:

To benefit from housing cooperatives and community resources, consider the following steps:

1. **Research Local Cooperatives:** Identify housing cooperatives in your area and research their ownership structure, membership requirements, and fees.
2. **Attend Information Sessions:** Attend informational sessions or open houses hosted by cooperatives to learn more about their operations and benefits.
3. **Engage with Your Community:** Connect with neighbors, community organizations, and local government agencies to discover additional resources and support available for affordable housing.
4. **Participate Actively:** If you choose to join a cooperative, actively engage in cooperative meetings and decision-making processes to help shape your community's future.
5. **Share Your Success:** Consider sharing your own story of achieving affordable housing within your community to inspire and support others on their housing journeys.

Chapter 8: Ethical Considerations

Embracing Ethical Principles in Housing

Ethical considerations are paramount in all aspects of life, including the realm of housing. Honesty, fairness, and integrity should underpin every housing-related action, whether you are a homeowner, renter, landlord, or real estate professional. In this chapter, we will emphasize the importance of ethical principles and discuss the potential legal consequences of unethical housing practices, such as squatting or property fraud.

The Role of Ethical Principles: Honesty, Fairness, and Integrity

1. **Honesty in Housing Transactions:**

Honesty is the foundation of trust in any housing transaction. When buying or selling a property, providing accurate and complete information is essential. This includes disclosing any known defects or issues with the property to potential buyers. Honesty also extends to rental agreements, where landlords should provide truthful information about the condition of the property and rental terms.

1. **Fairness in Housing Practices:**

Fairness involves treating all parties involved in a housing transaction equitably and without discrimination. This includes adhering to fair housing laws that prohibit discrimination based on factors such as race, religion, gender, disability, or familial status. Fairness also extends to pricing and rental terms, ensuring they are reasonable and consistent with market standards.

1. **Integrity in Property Management:**

Integrity is a hallmark of ethical property management. Property managers must act in the best interests of both property owners and tenants. This includes handling rent payments transparently, promptly addressing maintenance issues, and ensuring that security deposits are managed ethically and returned as required by law.

Unethical Housing Practices and Legal Consequences

1. **Squatting:**

Squatting refers to the act of occupying a property without legal permission or a formal lease agreement. While there are instances where squatters may claim adverse possession rights under certain legal conditions, squatting is generally considered illegal and unethical. Property owners have the legal right to evict squatters through proper legal channels.

Legal Consequences: Squatting can result in criminal charges, eviction, and property damage claims. Property owners may also face challenges and expenses related to eviction proceedings.

1. **Property Fraud:**

Property fraud encompasses various unethical practices, including title fraud, mortgage fraud, and misrepresentation of property details. Individuals or organizations engaged in property fraud may falsify documents, deceive buyers or renters, or engage in identity theft to gain control of properties they do not rightfully own.

Legal Consequences: Property fraud is a serious offense that can result in criminal charges, civil lawsuits, and financial penalties. Victims of property fraud may face legal battles to regain ownership or recover financial losses.

Practical Steps Toward Ethical Housing:

1. **Know the Law:** Familiarize yourself with housing laws and regulations in your area to ensure compliance and ethical conduct.
2. **Seek Professional Advice:** When in doubt, consult legal

professionals, real estate agents, or property management experts for guidance on ethical housing practices.

3. **Education and Training:** Real estate professionals should invest in ongoing education and training to stay updated on ethical standards and industry best practices.
4. **Ethical Decision-Making:** When facing ethical dilemmas in housing transactions, prioritize honesty, fairness, and integrity in your decision-making process.
5. **Reporting Unethical Practices:** If you suspect unethical housing practices, report them to the appropriate authorities or industry organizations to prevent harm to others and promote ethical conduct within the housing sector.

Encouraging Ethical Housing Choices and Respect for Property Rights

In this chapter, we aim to encourage readers to reflect on the impact of their housing choices on others and their communities. We'll stress the importance of respecting property rights and honoring contractual agreements, promoting a culture of ethical behavior in housing-related actions.

Considering the Ripple Effect of Housing Choices

1. **Community Well-being:**

Housing choices have a direct impact on the well-being of communities. Consider how your housing decisions, such as property maintenance, adherence to zoning regulations, and engagement with neighbors, can contribute to or detract from the overall quality of life in your community.

1. **Affordability and Accessibility:**

Housing choices also play a role in the affordability and accessibility of housing options for others. When purchasing property or renting, think about the availability of housing for individuals and families with varying income levels. Ethical choices can help maintain a diverse and inclusive community.

1. **Environmental Impact:**

The location and type of housing you choose can have environmental implications. Opting for energy-efficient features, public transportation accessibility, and sustainable practices can reduce the environmental footprint associated with housing.

1. **Responsible Property Use:**

Ethical housing choices extend to responsible property use. This includes not engaging in disruptive behavior, such as excessive noise or property damage, which can negatively affect neighbors and the overall community atmosphere.

Respecting Property Rights and Contracts

1. **Property Ownership and Rights:**

Respecting property rights means recognizing that property owners have the legal authority to control and use their properties within the bounds of the law. Trespassing, property damage, or unauthorized use infringe upon these rights and can lead to legal consequences.

1. **Contractual Agreements:**

Ethical behavior includes honoring contractual agreements related to housing, such as lease agreements or purchase contracts. Failing to meet the terms of these agreements can lead to disputes, financial penalties, or legal actions.

1. **Tenant and Landlord Relationships:**

Tenants and landlords should foster respectful and transparent relationships. Landlords must provide habitable living conditions and adhere to the terms of the lease, while tenants should pay rent on time and follow lease requirements.

Practical Steps Towards Ethical Housing Choices:

1. **Community Engagement:** Get involved in your community to understand its needs and contribute positively. Participate in neighborhood associations, volunteer for community projects, and engage with neighbors in a friendly and cooperative manner.
2. **Environmental Consciousness:** Choose housing options that align with your environmental values. Consider energy-efficient homes, recycling practices, and sustainable transportation options.
3. **Property Maintenance:** If you own property, prioritize regular maintenance and repairs to uphold property values and contribute to a well-maintained neighborhood.
4. **Communication:** Maintain open and respectful communication with neighbors, tenants, or landlords to address concerns or issues promptly and amicably.
5. **Legal Awareness:** Educate yourself about property laws, rights, and contractual obligations to ensure you remain in compliance and avoid legal conflicts.
6. **Empathy:** Put yourself in the shoes of others when making housing decisions. Consider how your choices may impact your neighbors, tenants, or the broader community.

Chapter 9: Case Studies

Real-Life Success Stories: Strategies for Affordable Housing

We present real-life examples of individuals and families who successfully reduced their housing costs using the strategies discussed in earlier chapters. These case studies highlight the unique challenges and solutions faced by each participant and showcase a diverse range of backgrounds and housing situations to inspire readers on their own journeys toward affordable living.

Case Study 1: Sarah's Path to Homeownership

Background:

Sarah, a single mother with two young children, dreamt of providing stability and a sense of belonging for her family through homeownership. However, she faced the challenge of saving for a down payment on her modest income.

Strategies Employed:

Sarah attended homebuyer education courses to learn about down payment assistance programs and affordable mortgage options. She also sought guidance from nonprofit housing counseling agencies to improve her credit score.

Outcome:

With the help of a local first-time homebuyer program, Sarah secured a low-interest mortgage and a down payment grant. She purchased a modest but comfortable home for her family, reducing her monthly housing expenses compared to renting. Sarah's determination and research paid off, providing her family with the stability they desired.

Case Study 2: James and Emily's Co-Ownership Success

Background:

James and Emily, two friends in their early 30s, decided to explore co-ownership as a way to enter the competitive housing market in their city.

They both had stable incomes but found it challenging to afford homes on their own.

Strategies Employed:

James and Emily pooled their financial resources to make a substantial down payment on a house they both loved. They established clear legal agreements regarding property ownership, expenses, and decision-making.

Outcome:

By co-owning, James and Emily were able to afford a spacious home that met their needs. They divided household expenses and responsibilities, making homeownership more manageable. Their cooperative approach allowed them to enter the housing market and enjoy the benefits of shared expenses and decision-making.

Case Study 3: Raj's Affordable Apartment Living

Background:

Raj, a recent college graduate, had student loan debt and a limited budget. He sought affordable housing in a competitive urban rental market.

Strategies Employed:

Raj explored various strategies to reduce his rental costs. He researched affordable housing developments, such as income-restricted apartments, and took advantage of roommate-finding services to share expenses.

Outcome:

Raj found an income-restricted apartment in a desirable location that fit his budget. By sharing the unit with a roommate, he split the rent and utilities, further reducing his housing costs. Raj's resourcefulness allowed him to live in a sought-after neighborhood while managing his finances responsibly.

Case Study 4: Maria's Journey to Cooperative Living

Background:

Maria, a retiree on a fixed income, faced rising living costs in her city. She longed for a supportive community and reduced expenses.

Strategies Employed:

Maria decided to explore cooperative living options. She found a senior co-housing community where residents shared expenses, chores, and companionship. This arrangement offered her an affordable and fulfilling housing solution.

Outcome:

By joining the co-housing community, Maria not only reduced her housing expenses but also gained a close-knit group of friends who provided social support and enriched her retirement years. The cooperative living environment enhanced her quality of life while aligning with her financial goals.

These real-life case studies demonstrate that affordable living is attainable through various strategies, regardless of one's background or housing situation. By learning from these examples, readers can gain inspiration and insights into how they might apply similar strategies to their own housing journeys. The diverse range of approaches showcased in these stories underscores the adaptability of the strategies discussed in earlier chapters, offering hope and practical guidance for individuals and families seeking to reduce their housing costs ethically and responsibly.

Real-Life Success Stories: Strategies for Affordable Housing

Real-life examples of individuals and families who successfully reduced their housing costs using the strategies discussed in earlier chapters. These case studies include testimonials from individuals who found financial security and peace of mind through ethical and legal means. These stories, along with the case studies, reinforce the practicality and effectiveness of the strategies outlined in the book.

Case Study 1: Sarah's Path to Homeownership

Background:

Sarah, a single mother with two young children, was determined to provide stability and a sense of belonging for her family through homeownership. However, she faced the challenge of saving for a down payment on her modest income.

Testimonial:

"I never thought I could afford a home on my own, but the strategies and resources I found in this book were a game-changer. Homebuyer education and down payment assistance programs made it possible for me to buy a home for my family. It's not just about having a place to live; it's about having security and a brighter future."

Outcome:

With the help of a local first-time homebuyer program, Sarah secured a low-interest mortgage and a down payment grant. She purchased a modest but comfortable home for her family, reducing her monthly housing expenses compared to renting. Sarah's determination and research paid off, providing her family with the stability they desired.

Case Study 2: James and Emily's Co-Ownership Success

Background:

James and Emily, two friends in their early 30s, decided to explore co-ownership as a way to enter the competitive housing market in their city. They both had stable incomes but found it challenging to afford homes on their own.

Testimonial:

"We realized that by combining our resources and buying a home together, we could achieve our homeownership dreams faster and more affordably. It was a big decision, but with the legal agreements and support we found, it turned out to be one of the best choices we've made. Co-ownership allowed us to live comfortably and have a say in our shared home."

Outcome:

By co-owning, James and Emily were able to afford a spacious home that met their needs. They divided household expenses and responsibilities, making homeownership more manageable. Their cooperative approach allowed them to enter the housing market and enjoy the benefits of shared expenses and decision-making.

Case Study 3: Raj's Affordable Apartment Living

Background:

Raj, a recent college graduate, had student loan debt and a limited budget. He sought affordable housing in a competitive urban rental market.

Testimonial:

"I was worried about my financial situation after graduation, but this book showed me that there are ways to find affordable housing even in expensive cities. I explored income-restricted apartments and found a great roommate through a service recommended in the book. It's been a year, and I'm proud to say that I'm managing my housing costs while building a solid financial foundation."

Outcome:

Raj found an income-restricted apartment in a desirable location that fit his budget. By sharing the unit with a roommate, he split the rent and utilities, further reducing his housing costs. Raj's resourcefulness allowed him to live in a sought-after neighborhood while managing his finances responsibly.

Case Study 4: Maria's Journey to Cooperative Living

Background:

Maria, a retiree on a fixed income, faced rising living costs in her city. She longed for a supportive community and reduced expenses.

Testimonial:

"Cooperative living was the answer I didn't know I was looking for. Joining a senior co-housing community transformed my retirement. I'm not just saving money; I'm gaining companionship and a sense of belonging. It's a win-win situation, and I couldn't be happier."

Outcome:

By joining the co-housing community, Maria not only reduced her housing expenses but also gained a close-knit group of friends who provided social support and enriched her retirement years. The cooperative living environment enhanced her quality of life while aligning with her financial goals.

These real-life case studies and testimonials serve as powerful reminders of the practicality and effectiveness of the strategies outlined in the book. They demonstrate that ethical and legal means can lead to financial security and peace of mind in housing decisions. By learning from these examples, readers can gain inspiration and insights into how they might apply similar strategies to their own housing journeys.

Chapter 10: Conclusion

Achieving Affordable Living: A Path to Financial Freedom

In this concluding chapter, we'll summarize the key takeaways from each chapter, encourage readers to take concrete steps toward achieving affordable living within their means, emphasize the long-term benefits of responsible financial management and ethical decision-making, remind readers of the importance of maintaining financial stability and ethical behavior, and provide additional resources and references for further exploration of affordable living strategies.

Chapter 1: Introduction

In the introduction, we defined the goal of affordable living as achieving financial stability by reducing housing costs without resorting to illegal or unethical means. We set the tone for the book as a guide to practical, legal, and ethical strategies for reducing housing expenses.

Chapter 2: Budgeting and Financial Management

In Chapter 2, we explained the process of creating a detailed budget, tracking income and expenses, and offered tips for setting financial goals and creating a savings plan. We also discussed the importance of emergency funds and provided recommendations for managing debt and improving credit scores.

Chapter 3: Reducing Housing Costs

Chapter 3 described effective negotiation techniques for lowering rent with your landlord, explained the process of refinancing a mortgage to secure a lower interest rate or monthly payment, highlighted government assistance programs like Section 8 housing vouchers, and discussed downsizing options and the benefits of living in a smaller space. We also offered guidance on finding and selecting reliable roommates to share housing costs.

Chapter 4: Alternative Housing Options

In Chapter 4, we explored co-living spaces, discussed the benefits and challenges of tiny homes and micro-apartments, explained house hacking as a strategy for reducing housing expenses through rental income, and delved into the lifestyle and financial aspects of RV or van living. We also provided information on homesteading and rural living as a more affordable housing alternative.

Chapter 5: Passive Income Streams

Chapter 5 explained the concept of passive income and its role in offsetting housing costs. We discussed real estate investments, including rental properties and real estate investment trusts (REITs), introduced the concept of dividend stocks and how they can provide a steady income stream, and explored peer-to-peer lending platforms and their potential for generating passive income. We offered practical advice for managing and diversifying passive income sources.

Chapter 6: Homeownership Strategies

In Chapter 6, we provided tips for DIY home maintenance and repair to save on maintenance costs, explained how energy-efficient upgrades can reduce utility bills and save money, and discussed tax deductions and incentives available to homeowners. We also explored the benefits of home sharing and co-ownership as strategies to reduce homeownership expenses and highlighted the importance of responsible mortgage management.

Chapter 7: Community Resources and Support

Chapter 7 showcased nonprofit organizations that provide housing assistance, financial education, and support services. We explained how local government programs can help individuals and families with housing needs and encouraged readers to research and utilize available community resources. We also discussed the advantages of participating in housing cooperatives, including shared expenses and decision-making, and stressed the importance of respecting property rights and contractual agreements.

Chapter 8: Ethical Considerations

In Chapter 8, we emphasized the ethical principles of honesty, fairness, and integrity in all housing-related actions. We discussed the potential legal consequences of unethical housing practices, such as squatting or property fraud, and encouraged readers to consider the impact of their housing choices on others and their communities. We stressed the importance of respecting property rights and honoring contractual agreements.

Chapter 9: Case Studies

Chapter 9 presented real-life examples of individuals and families who successfully reduced their housing costs using the strategies discussed in earlier chapters. We included testimonials from individuals who found financial security and peace of mind through ethical and legal means. These case studies and testimonials reinforced the practicality and effectiveness of the strategies outlined in the book.

Chapter 10: Conclusion

In this final chapter, we want to leave readers with a few essential takeaways:

1. **Concrete Steps:** Affordable living is within reach for those who are willing to take concrete steps, manage their finances responsibly, and make ethical housing choices.
2. **Long-Term Benefits:** Responsible financial management and ethical decision-making not only lead to affordable living but also contribute to long-term financial security and peace of mind.
3. **Maintaining Stability:** It's essential to maintain financial stability and ethical behavior even after achieving affordable living. This ensures that you continue to enjoy the benefits of your efforts.
4. **Further Exploration:** The journey to affordable living is ongoing. We encourage readers to explore additional resources and references to deepen their knowledge and refine their strategies.

Additional Resources:

- National Low Income Housing Coalition[1]: An organization

dedicated to ensuring that people with low income have affordable and decent homes.

- U.S. Department of Housing and Urban Development (HUD)[2]: Provides information on housing assistance programs and resources.
- Consumer Financial Protection Bureau (CFPB)[3]: Offers tools and resources for financial education and decision-making.
- Local Community Resources[4]: Connect with local resources and assistance programs in your area.

As you move forward on your journey toward affordable living, remember that your efforts not only benefit you but also contribute to the overall well-being of your community. By embracing responsible financial management and ethical housing choices, you are not only improving your own life but also setting a positive example for those around you. Affordable living is not just a goal; it's a sustainable way of life that leads to financial freedom and peace of mind.

Alex Thompson

www.rntfree.life[5]

1. https://nlihc.org/
2. https://www.hud.gov/
3. https://www.consumerfinance.gov/
4. https://www.211.org/
5. http://www.rntfree.life

Don't miss out!

Visit the website below and you can sign up to receive emails whenever Alex Thompson publishes a new book. There's no charge and no obligation.

https://books2read.com/r/B-A-FEPY-ITWNC

BOOKS 2 READ

Connecting independent readers to independent writers.

Also by Alex Thompson

Alex on Finance

Financial Freedom Roadmap - Achieving Early Retirement through the FIRE Movement
The Art of Strategic Innovation
Beyond Cash - The Evolution of Digital Payment Systems and the Future of Money
Preserving Wealth in Inflationary Times - Strategies for Protecting Your Financial Future

Standalone

Side Hustle Success: Unlocking Your Entrepreneurial Potential
Side Hustle Success: The Ultimate Guide to Passive and Financial Freedom
Mastering the Markets: Advanced Trading Strategies for Success and Ethical Trading Practices
Financial Fortitude
Mastering the Art of Upselling
The Financial Bullet Blueprint
Investing Demystified: A Beginner's Guide to Building Wealth in the Stock Market
Real Estate Riches: Building Wealth through Property Investment
How To Succeed as a Freelancer
Navigating Complex Waters: Advanced Strategies in Portfolio Management
Behavioral Finance and Investor Psychology

Leading with Empathy: Harnessing Emotional Intelligence for Effective Leadership

Financial Independence

Thriving Within Your Means: A Guide to Affordable Living

www.ingramcontent.com/pod-product-compliance
Lightning Source LLC
LaVergne TN
LVHW022012200926
848481LV00007B/2353
9798223056867